Table of Contents

DEDICATION...3

PREFACE...6

INTRODUCTION..8

Category 1: Manhood & Identity...........................10

Category 2: Brotherhood..................................37

Category 3: Fatherhood...................................66

Category 4: Marriage & Devotion..........................94

Category 5: Leadership..................................123

Category 6: Work & Provision............................152

Category 7: Physical Discipline.........................181

Category 8: Mental Toughness............................204

Category 9: Legacy & Purpose............................234

Category 10: Faith & Spiritual Warfare..................261

CONCLUSION..286

Appendix A: Scripture Foundations.......................287

Appendix B: Recommended Reading.........................288

Appendix C: Complete Index of Lists.....................288

THE FORGOTTEN STANDARDS FOR MEN

Standards the World Forgot — and the Men Who Carry Them Anyway

by Geoffrey Arbuckle

CANE Enterprises Publishing, LLC

Copyright © 2026 by Geoffrey Arbuckle

All rights reserved. No part of this publication may be reproduced, distributed, or transmitted in any form or by any means, including photocopying, recording, or other electronic or mechanical methods, without the prior written permission of the publisher, except in the case of brief quotations embodied in critical reviews and certain other noncommercial uses permitted by copyright law.

Published by CANE Enterprises Publishing, LLC Kansas City, Missouri

Unless otherwise noted, all Scripture quotations are from the Holy Bible, New International Version®, NIV®. Copyright © 1973, 1978, 1984, 2011 by Biblica, Inc.™ Used by permission. All rights reserved worldwide.

Scripture quotations marked KJV are from the King James Version of the Bible.

ISBN-13 (eBook): 979-8-9957319-2-4

ISBN-13 (Paperback): 979-8-9957319-3-1

ISBN-13 (Hardcover): 979-8-9957319-4-8

Printed in the United States of America

First Edition

DEDICATION

For my father, Chris Arbuckle —

You are my North Star. The fixed point by which I have always taken my bearings. The anchor that held when everything else was moving.

You were my father. Not my friend. I thank God for the distinction. You loved me enough to do the harder thing — to set the standard rather than lower it, to correct me rather than flatter me, to tell me the truth when a lie would have been easier for both of us.

You poured yourself out. Your time. Your energy. Your attention. Your sacrifice. Decades of it, most of it unseen, none of it owed. Every hour you gave me came from somewhere else you could have spent it. I know that now.

Before I could put these standards into words, I had already seen them lived. Before I could defend them, I had already been loved by them. Every page of this book is something I learned first by watching you.

I am the man I am today because you chose, day after day, to be the man you were. Whatever integrity I carry, whatever faith I hold, whatever steadiness I bring to my own family — I learned it from you.

Thank you, Dad.

For my brothers, Christopher and Gregory Arbuckle —

You have known me longer than almost anyone. You saw me before I knew who I was. You watched me fall and stand up and fall again — and you never used what you saw against me. Few men are given that kind of witness. Fewer still are given it twice.

You carry the same name I do. You carry the same standards. When I look at either of you I see a man who chose faith over ease, family over ambition, and brotherhood over whatever the world was selling at the time.

Thank you for being the kind of brothers a man can measure himself against. Thank you for being the kind of brothers a man can rest in.

For China Polly Arbuckle, my wife —

You saw me at my darkest hour and did not look away. You held on when letting go would have been easier — for you and for anyone else. You believed me when I said I could build something, then you stayed up with me while I built it.

A man's character is tested by what he does when no one is watching. His wife is the one who is always watching. That you still love me is a mercy I did not earn. That you still stand beside me is a grace I will spend the rest of my life trying to be worthy of.

This book is a record of standards I learned slowly. You already knew them all. You just lived them, waiting for me to catch up.

❦

For my children — John Chandler, Blake Anthony, Madison Nicole, and William Edwin —

Everything your grandfather taught me, I am trying to teach you. Everything I did not learn in time, I am learning now, for your sake.

To my sons: this book was written with you in the room. Every standard in it is one I want engraved on your bones before the world gets a chance to talk you out of them. Be men who know who you are. Be men who protect, who provide, who kneel. Be the kind of men your children can one day say what I am saying now about my father.

To my daughter, Madison: this book is about what a real man looks like — and you have already found him. His name is Ben Steven, and what is true of him in these pages was true of him before he ever read them. Whatever wisdom about men a father can hand his daughter is here, but the truth is you will recognize most of it. May the standards in this book hold for you both — for you, Madison, and for you, Ben — all the days of your marriage.

I love you. All four of you. More than I know how to say.

PREFACE

This book was not written from a place of comfort.

It was written by a man who had his neck broken at twenty by a drunk driver who never stopped. A man who lost his sight years later in a moment of unbearable darkness. A man who has stood in the wreckage of things he thought would last forever and watched them fall.

I did not write this book because I have mastered the standards within it. I wrote it because I have been broken by their absence — in my own life and in the lives of the men around me.

We live in a world that has lost its definition of manhood. On one side, men are told that strength means dominance, that authority means control, that masculinity is measured by volume and force. On the other side, men are told to shrink — to apologize for their strength, to suppress their instincts, to become a softer version of something the world can manage.

Both are lies.

The man this book was written for is neither the tyrant nor the doormat. He is the man who leads by serving. Who protects without controlling. Who fights by kneeling first. Who can weep without shame and stand without apology. Who measures his strength not by what he conquers but by what he builds, what he guards, and who he becomes when no one is watching.

He is the man Christ modeled — the One who flipped tables in the temple and washed the feet of His followers. Who wept openly at the grave of His friend and walked willingly into His own death. That is not a weak man. That is not a dangerous man. That is the standard.

This book contains one hundred lists across ten categories that cover every arena of a man's life: his identity, his friendships, his children, his marriage, his leadership, his work, his body, his mind, his legacy, and his faith. Each list contains ten items — direct, biblical, and forged in the fire of personal experience. Each category concludes with ten quotes from history's wisest voices and ten actionable steps to begin putting these standards into practice immediately.

It is not a book about what the culture celebrates. It is a book about what God requires. And the distance between those two things is the distance most men spend their entire lives trying to close.

If you are a young man trying to figure out who you are — this book is for you. If you are a husband trying to love your wife the way she deserves — this book is for you. If you are a father trying not to repeat the mistakes your father made — this book is for you. If you are an older man wondering whether the second half of your life can be better than the first — this book is for you.

The standards in this book are not new. They are ancient. They have always been true. The world simply forgot them.

It's time to remember.

— Geoffrey Arbuckle

INTRODUCTION

The world has a man problem.

Not because men are too strong. Because they are too lost.

A generation of men is drowning in silence — scrolling through screens at midnight instead of sleeping beside their wives. Pouring their best energy into jobs that will replace them and their leftover scraps into families that won't. Building kingdoms out of ambition and watching them crumble because the foundation was made of ego instead of character.

They don't know who they are. They don't know what they believe. And the voices they're listening to — the ones on the screen, the ones in the algorithm, the ones that promise power without sacrifice and leadership without service — are leading them off a cliff while selling them tickets to the view.

This book is not another voice in the noise.

It is a return to the signal.

The signal is ancient. It is biblical. It is proven across centuries of men who lived by a standard the modern world has abandoned. It requires strength — real strength, the kind that holds its tongue when provoked and speaks up when injustice demands it. It requires gentleness — real gentleness, the kind that carries a child with the same hands that carry the burden. It requires faith — real faith, the kind that kneels before it stands and trusts before it sees.

This book is organized into ten categories:

Manhood & Identity
Brotherhood
Fatherhood
Marriage & Devotion
Leadership
Work & Provision
Physical Discipline
Mental Toughness
Legacy & Purpose
Faith & Spiritual Warfare

Each category contains ten lists of ten items — one hundred lists, one thousand truths. Each category concludes with ten quotes and ten practice steps designed to move these truths from the page into your daily life.

You don't have to read it in order. Open to the category that's calling your name. Start with the list that addresses what you're facing today. But read it with a pen. Mark what hits you. Come back to it. Let it shape you.

This is not a book about what's popular. It's a book about what's true.

And what's true has never gone out of style. The world just stopped teaching it.

Until now.

CATEGORY 1

MANHOOD & IDENTITY

List 1: Ten Marks of a Man Who Knows Who He Is

He doesn't need the room to validate him. — A man who knows who he is can walk into any room — boardroom, locker room, living room — and not adjust his personality to match the crowd. He is the same man everywhere because he isn't performing for anyone. The need to be liked is the first thing a real man buries.

He has been tested and did not break. — Identity isn't forged in comfort. It's forged in fire. A man who knows who he is has stood in the middle of something that should have destroyed him — a loss, a betrayal, a failure so deep it rewrote his plans — and came out the other side still standing. He doesn't talk about it to impress people. He carries it quietly, and it shows.

He keeps his word even when it costs him. — His yes means yes. His no means no. He doesn't make promises he can't keep, and when he makes one he shouldn't have, he keeps it anyway. A man's word is either the foundation everything else is built on or the crack that brings the whole house down.

He protects without controlling. — He covers the people he loves. He watches the door. He walks her to the car. He checks on the kids at night. But he doesn't confuse protection with possession. He guards without gripping. He leads without leashing. The difference between a protector and a tyrant is whether the people around him feel safe or suffocated.

He can sit in silence without reaching for a screen. — A man who knows who he is doesn't need constant noise to drown out what's inside. He can sit on a porch, drive in a car, or lie in bed without the reflexive grab for a device. Silence doesn't terrify him because he's not running from himself. Most men are — and the screens are just the fastest way to avoid the mirror.

He admits when he's wrong without falling apart. — Ego makes a man double down. Identity lets him own it. A man who knows himself can say, "I was wrong. I'm sorry. I'll do better," without treating it like a defeat. The strongest men in any room are the ones who don't need to be right every time to feel like they matter.

He defines success on his own terms. — He stopped measuring his life by another man's yardstick a long time ago. The house, the car, the title — those are fine, but they're not the scoreboard. A man who knows who he is measures himself by how present he is in his children's lives, how loved his wife feels, how much he gave versus how much he took. Everything else is decoration.

He does not confuse volume with authority. — The loudest voice in the room is almost never the strongest. A man who knows who he is speaks with weight, not decibels. He doesn't need to shout over people to be heard. When he does speak, the room listens — not because they're afraid, but because they know he doesn't waste words.

He is comfortable being disliked. — Not everyone will understand him. Not everyone will approve of his convictions, his boundaries, or his faith. A man who knows who he is has made peace with that. He would rather be respected by the few who matter than applauded by the many who don't. Popularity is a poor substitute for purpose.

He treats every man with dignity regardless of rank. — He looks the janitor in the eye and shakes his hand the same way he shakes the CEO's. He doesn't adjust his kindness based on what someone can do for him. A man who knows who he is doesn't measure people by position. He measures them by character — and he extends his own to everyone.

List 2: Ten Lies the World Tells Men About Masculinity

"Real men don't cry." — This lie has buried more men than any war. Grief unexpressed becomes rage. Pain swallowed becomes addiction. The strongest men in history wept openly — David wept, Jesus wept, warriors wept over fallen brothers. Tears are not weakness. They are proof that something inside you still works.

"Your value is your paycheck." — The world will tell you that your worth as a man is measured in what you earn. It's a lie designed to keep you working yourself to death while your family learns to live without you.

Provision matters. But a man who gives his children everything except himself has provided nothing that lasts.

"Vulnerability is a liability." — The man who never lets anyone in will die surrounded by people who never really knew him. Vulnerability is not broadcasting your wounds on the internet. It is sitting across from your wife, your brother, your son, and telling the truth about where you are. That takes more courage than any mask you've ever worn.

"You should be able to handle it on your own." — No man was built to carry everything alone. The lie of self-sufficiency has produced a generation of men who are drowning in silence because they believe asking for help is the same as admitting defeat. It's not. It's admitting you're human. And the men who survive this life are the ones who had other men standing beside them.

"If you're not winning, you're losing." — Life is not a scoreboard. Not every season is a victory lap, and not every setback is a failure. Some of the best men you will ever meet are in the middle of the hardest years of their lives, and they're still showing up. That's not losing. That's enduring. And endurance is what separates the men who last from the men who flame out.

"More is always better." — More money. More power. More followers. More stimulation. The world feeds men a lie that contentment is the enemy of ambition. It's not. Contentment is the ability to sit in what you have and know it's enough — while still working toward what's next. The man chasing more never stops to realize he already has what matters.

"Anger is strength." — Anger is easy. Any man can explode. It takes no discipline, no restraint, no character. Real strength is the man who feels the fire and controls it. Who absorbs the insult and doesn't return it. Who walks away from the fight he could win because winning it would cost more than it's worth. Rage is not power. It's proof that something else has power over you.

"A man's body is his own." — Your body is not yours alone. It belongs to the wife who sleeps beside you, the children who climb on your back, the friends who need you at seventy. What you put into it, what you do with it, and how you maintain it is not a personal choice — it is a stewardship. Treat it like a rental and you'll return it wrecked.

"Faith is for the weak." — The men who say this have usually never been truly broken. They've never stood at the edge of something so dark that their strength couldn't reach the other side. Faith is not a crutch. It is the only thing that holds when everything man-made fails. The bravest men in history were not the ones who stood alone. They were the ones who knelt first.

"You can have it all." — You can't. Every yes is a no to something else. Every late night at the office is a bedtime story you didn't read. Every weekend with the boys is a Saturday your wife spent alone. A man of wisdom doesn't chase everything. He chooses what matters most and gives it everything he has. That's not limitation. That's focus.

List 3: Ten Ways to Define Yourself Before the World Does It for You

Write down what you believe and why. — Most men have never done this. They carry inherited beliefs, borrowed opinions, and cultural assumptions they've never examined. Sit down with a blank page and write out what you believe about God, family, work, manhood, death, and purpose. If you can't articulate it, you don't own it yet.

Identify the three people whose opinion actually matters to you. — Not the internet. Not your coworkers. Not the algorithm. Choose three people — your wife, your mentor, your closest brother — and let their voices carry weight. Everyone else is noise. When you stop living for the crowd, you start living for what's real.

Decide what you will not do, no matter what. — Every man needs a line he will not cross. Not a vague moral sentiment but a concrete list. Write it down. I will not lie to my wife. I will not hit my children in anger. I will not sacrifice my integrity for a promotion. These are not aspirations. They are the walls of your house. Without them, anything can walk in.

Spend time alone without a device. — You cannot know yourself if you are never alone with yourself. The constant stream of content, notification, and noise exists to keep you from thinking. Turn it off. Go for a walk. Sit in a room. Drive without the radio. The man you are is the man you meet in the silence — and most men have been avoiding that introduction for years.

Study the men you admire and identify what you see in them. — Not celebrities. Not influencers. Men you know — or men from history — who lived with integrity, loved their families, served their communities, and died with clean hands. What did they have in common? That's your blueprint. You become what you study. Choose carefully.

Accept the parts of your story you cannot change. — Your father left. Your childhood was hard. Your first marriage failed. Your body broke. A man who defines himself is not a man without scars. He is a man who has stopped letting the scars write the narrative. Your past is a chapter. It is not the whole book — unless you keep rereading it.

Reject the labels other people have assigned to you. — Stupid. Lazy. Not good enough. Too much. Too little. Someone said it — maybe a parent, maybe a coach, maybe an ex — and you've been wearing it ever since. Take it off. Those words were spoken by broken people from broken places. They do not define you unless you let them.

Choose your habits before your habits choose you. — You are not what you intend. You are what you do repeatedly. The man who scrolls for two hours every night is not a man who values presence — no matter what he says. The man who gets up early to pray, to read, to move his body — that man is building something. Identity is not declared. It is built, one discipline at a time.

Tell the truth about your weaknesses before someone else exposes them. — Every man has them. The ones who define themselves are the ones who name them first. I struggle with anger. I check out when things get hard. I drink more than I should. Naming it is not defeat. It is the first step toward owning it — and owning it is the first step toward changing it.

Live in a way that your children could follow and be proud. — If your son lived exactly the way you live — scrolled what you scroll, spoke how you speak, treated women the way you treat women — would you be proud of him? If your daughter married a man exactly like you, would you be at peace? That is the mirror. Look into it. Then decide who you want to be.

List 4: Ten Things Every Man Should Know by the Time He's Thirty

How to control his temper. — By thirty, a man should have learned the difference between feeling anger and acting on it. The boy throws things, punches walls, raises his voice to win arguments. The man breathes. Pauses. Responds instead of reacts. If you haven't learned this by thirty, you will spend the next decade cleaning up damage that didn't need to happen.

How to apologize without making excuses. — "I'm sorry, but—" is not an apology. It is a defense wrapped in polite clothing. By thirty, a man should know how to say, "I was wrong. I hurt you. There is no excuse." Period. No qualifiers, no redirects, no blame-shifting. A clean apology is one of the most powerful things a man can offer — and one of the rarest.

How to manage money. — Not how to make it. How to manage it. How to budget, save, give, and live below his means. A man who earns six figures and spends seven is not successful. He's a slave with a nice car. By thirty, a man should understand that financial discipline is not about deprivation — it's about freedom.

How to listen without waiting to talk. — Most men listen the way they drive — aggressively, looking for an opening. By thirty, a man should have learned that silence is not a gap to be filled. Sometimes the most powerful thing you can do is close your mouth, look someone in the eye, and let them finish. Your wife needs this. Your children need this. Your friends need this.

What he believes about God and why. — A borrowed faith will not survive a real crisis. By thirty, a man should have wrestled with the big questions — not just inherited his parents' answers. Whether he lands on his knees or walks away, he should have done the work. A man who has never questioned his faith has never truly owned it.

How to be alone without being lonely. — Solitude is a skill. By thirty, a man should be able to spend time with himself — not numbed by a screen, not distracted by noise, not running from his own thoughts. A man who cannot sit with himself will never be fully present with anyone else. Learn to be still. It will save your life later.

How to have a hard conversation without destroying the relationship. — By thirty, you will have had to say things no one wants to hear. To a friend who's making a mistake. To a wife who's hurting. To a parent who let you down. The ability to speak truth without cruelty — to be honest without being brutal — is one of the defining marks of a grown man.

How to take care of his body. — Not to look impressive. To last. By thirty, a man should know how to feed himself well, move his body with intention, sleep like it matters, and stop treating his health as something he'll deal with later. Later comes faster than any man expects.

That his father's failures do not have to become his own. — By thirty, a man should have come to terms with the fact that his father was a man, not a god — and that whatever his father got wrong does not have to be the blueprint. You can honor a flawed man without repeating his mistakes. You can grieve what you didn't get without letting it define what you give.

That the world does not owe him anything. — Not a career. Not a wife. Not respect. Not comfort. By thirty, a man should have buried the entitlement that says, "I deserve this because I exist." What you get in this life is built, earned, given by grace, or lost by neglect. The sooner a man accepts that, the sooner he starts building something real.

List 5: Ten Ways to Be Strong Without Being Dangerous

Speak with conviction, not contempt. — Strong men have opinions. Dangerous men weaponize them. Say what you believe with clarity and confidence, but never with the intent to wound. The moment your words are designed to humiliate rather than communicate, you've stopped being strong and started being cruel.

Use your physical presence to protect, not to intimidate. — A strong man walks into a room and people feel safe. A dangerous man walks into a room and people feel small. The difference is not in his size. It's in his intention. Stand tall, move with purpose, and let your presence be a shelter — not a threat.

Control your anger instead of excusing it. — "That's just how I am" is not a reason. It's a resignation. A strong man feels the full weight of his anger and chooses what to do with it. He channels it toward change, toward protection, toward work that matters. A dangerous man lets it leak out on the people closest to him and calls it honesty.

Be competitive without being ruthless. — There is nothing wrong with wanting to win. But there is everything wrong with needing to win so badly that you'll step on anyone in your way. Compete hard. Play to your limits. Then shake the man's hand when it's over — win or lose. A strong man can lose with dignity. A dangerous man cannot.

Know when to fight and when to walk away. — Strength is not the willingness to fight. It's the wisdom to know which fights are worth it. A dangerous man fights every battle because he can. A strong man fights only the battles that matter — the ones that protect his family, his integrity, or someone who can't protect themselves.

Let your wife disagree with you without punishing her for it. — A strong man can hear his wife's opposing opinion and not take it as a personal attack. He can listen, consider, and even change his mind without losing his sense of authority. A dangerous man treats disagreement as disrespect — and the people around him learn to stay silent.

Hold power loosely. — Whether it's at work, in the home, or in the church — the most dangerous men are the ones who grip power like it defines them. A strong man holds it like a tool, not a trophy. He uses it to serve, and he's willing to set it down when the time comes. Power reveals a man's character faster than anything else.

Be honest without being harsh. — "I'm just being real" has become the excuse of every man who lacks the discipline to tell the truth with kindness. Strong men are honest. Dangerous men are brutal and call it honesty. The truth doesn't need a fist behind it. Say it plainly, say it with respect, and let it stand on its own.

Discipline your children without humiliating them. — A strong father corrects. A dangerous father shames. The difference between the two is not the discipline itself — it's whether your child walks away feeling corrected or feeling worthless. Discipline builds. Humiliation destroys. Know the difference, and your children will never fear your love.

Let people see your gentleness. — The strongest men in the world are gentle with children, tender with the elderly, kind to animals, and present with the hurting. Gentleness is not softness. It is controlled strength — power that knows when to pull back. A man who is only hard has not yet learned the highest form of strength.

List 6: Ten Ways to Be Gentle Without Being Weak

Hold your child like the world outside doesn't exist. — When your son or daughter crawls into your lap, put the phone down. Put the thoughts down. Be there — all of you. Gentleness with your children is not a performance. It is a deposit into a trust account that will pay dividends for the rest of their lives. The man who holds his children well raises children who hold the world well.

Speak softly to your wife when you're frustrated. — The natural reaction is to raise your voice. The disciplined reaction is to lower it. A man who can disagree with his wife in a tone that doesn't frighten her has mastered something most men never will. Softness in conflict is not surrender. It is the refusal to let the moment become bigger than the marriage.

Let someone else take the credit. — Weak men need recognition. Gentle men don't. If your team wins, point to them. If your family thrives, point to your wife. The man who constantly draws attention to his own contribution hasn't learned that real leadership is invisible — it does its work and disappears.

Sit with someone in pain without trying to fix it. — Men are wired to solve. But sometimes the strongest thing you can do is shut up and sit down. Your friend lost his mother. Your wife had a terrible day. Your son failed at something that mattered to him. Don't lecture. Don't strategize. Just be there. Presence is one of the most generous things a man can offer.

Serve without being asked. — Do the dishes. Mow the neighbor's lawn. Pick up the groceries. Not because someone told you to, but because you saw the need and met it. A gentle man doesn't wait for instructions to be kind. He moves toward the gap. And he doesn't need a thank-you to feel good about it.

Forgive someone who doesn't deserve it. — This is where gentleness separates from weakness. Weakness avoids the confrontation. Gentleness absorbs the injury, processes the pain, and releases the debt. Forgiveness doesn't mean what they did was acceptable. It means you've decided that carrying it is no longer yours to bear. That's not weakness. That's war — against the bitterness that would otherwise destroy you.

Touch gently. — A hand on your wife's back when she's stressed. A hand on your son's shoulder when he's scared. A hug that lasts one beat longer than usual. Men underestimate the power of gentle touch because the world has taught them to associate touch with force. But the man who touches with care is the man whose family feels safe in his hands.

Admit when you don't know. — "I don't know" is one of the most honest — and most gentle — things a man can say. It opens the door for learning, for collaboration, for humility. The man who pretends to know everything is performing. The man who admits what he doesn't know is building trust. And trust outlasts every performance.

Be patient with people who are slower than you. — Not everyone thinks at your speed, works at your pace, or processes at your rate. Gentleness means giving people room to be who they are without pressuring them to be who you are. Your wife doesn't have to respond to conflict the way you do. Your child doesn't have to learn at the speed you expect. Patience is gentleness stretched across time.

Choose your battles and surrender the rest. — A weak man surrenders everything because he's afraid of conflict. A gentle man surrenders the things that don't matter because he knows where his energy belongs. Not every disagreement is a hill to die on. Not every slight needs a response. The gentle man fights for what matters and lets the rest fall away. That's not weakness. That's wisdom.

List 7: Ten Ways to Kill the Boy and Let the Man Live

Stop blaming your parents for who you are today. — They failed you. Maybe badly. That's real, and it matters. But at some point, the explanation becomes an excuse — and the excuse becomes a cage. The boy says, "I am this way because of them." The man says, "I was shaped by them, but I am not sentenced by them." Take the keys. Walk out. Build something different.

Put away the things that keep you numb. — The boy reaches for the bottle, the screen, the fantasy, the feed — anything to avoid the discomfort of being fully present in his own life. The man puts those things down, even when they're calling, and sits in the discomfort long enough to learn what it's trying to teach him. Numbness is not peace. It is avoidance wearing comfortable clothes.

Make decisions and live with the consequences. — The boy waits to be told what to do. He hedges, delays, and looks for someone else to take the blame if it goes wrong. The man assesses, decides, and moves — knowing that some decisions will be wrong and that wrong decisions made with integrity are still better than no decisions made at all.

Keep your commitments even when you don't feel like it. — The boy is governed by feelings. He shows up when he's inspired and disappears when he's not. The man shows up because he said he would. He goes to the job, the marriage, the church, the friendship — not because he always wants to, but because his word is worth more than his mood.

Stop chasing approval from people who don't matter. — The boy curates his life for an audience. He adjusts his opinions, his appearance, and his values to match whatever crowd he's standing in. The man settled that question years ago. He knows who he is, who he answers to, and whose opinion carries weight. Everyone else can take it or leave it.

Learn to be bored. — The boy cannot handle boredom. He fills every gap with noise — scrolling, swiping, consuming, anything to avoid the terrifying silence of an unoccupied mind. The man has learned that boredom is not the enemy. It is the doorway to reflection, creativity, prayer, and self-awareness. If you cannot sit still for thirty minutes without reaching for a screen, the boy is still running things.

Take responsibility for your home. — The boy lives in someone else's structure. The man builds his own. That means leading your family, not just funding it. It means knowing what your wife needs and providing it. It means knowing what your children are struggling with and addressing it. It means being the thermostat, not the thermometer — setting the temperature instead of reacting to it.

Stop competing with other men for things that don't matter. — The boy measures himself by the car he drives, the weight he lifts, the woman on his arm. The man stopped keeping that kind of score years ago. He competes with himself — with yesterday's version of who he was — and measures his progress by whether he is becoming more faithful, more present, more useful, more kind.

Have the conversations you've been avoiding. — The boy ghosts. The man shows up. If there's a relationship that needs repair, repair it. If there's a truth that needs to be spoken, speak it. If there's an apology that needs to be made, make it. The boy puts it off because it's uncomfortable. The man walks into the discomfort because integrity demands it.

Accept that comfort is not the goal. — The boy organizes his life around ease. The man organizes his life around purpose — and purpose is rarely comfortable. Growth hurts. Discipline costs. Love demands sacrifice. The man who chooses comfort over calling will wake up one day and realize he built a very comfortable prison.

List 8: Ten Standards Every Man Should Refuse to Lower

Tell the truth, even when the lie would be easier. — Honesty is the floor, not the ceiling. A man who lies to avoid consequences is a man who has traded his integrity for convenience. The truth may cost you a friendship, a promotion, or a comfortable evening — but it will never cost you your self-respect. Once that's gone, everything else is theater.

Show up for your family, no matter how tired you are. — The world will drain you. Your job will drain you. Life will drain you. And when you walk through that door exhausted, your family will still be standing there — needing you. Not a better paycheck. You. A man who is present in body but absent in spirit has already left the building. Show up fully or don't pretend.

Treat every woman with respect. — Not because she earned it. Because you're a man and that's what men do. In how you speak, how you look, how you act — on the screen and off it. Every woman is someone's daughter, someone's mother, someone's sister. The standard is not "how much can I get away with." The standard is honor. Period.

Keep your body as a tool, not a toy. — What you consume, how you move, what you put in — these are not preferences. They are responsibilities. A man who lets his body fall apart while his children are still growing is a man who has chosen comfort over duty. You don't have to be an athlete. You have to be available. For decades.

Refuse to gossip. — If you wouldn't say it to his face, don't say it behind his back. Gossip is cowardice in casual clothing. A man of standard talks about ideas, not people. And when someone brings another man's name into the room to tear it down, a man of standard changes the subject — or leaves the room.

Protect your marriage from every threat. — Not just from affairs. From the slow erosion of neglect, distraction, selfishness, and laziness. From the screen that gets more of your attention than your wife. From the friendships that pull you away instead of pushing you closer. A marriage doesn't die in a moment. It dies in a thousand unguarded ones.

Do not take what isn't yours. — Not another man's wife. Not another man's credit. Not another man's opportunity. Not a dollar that doesn't belong to you. A man who takes what isn't his reveals what he actually thinks of himself — that he isn't capable of building his own. Earn it. Build it. Or go without. But never steal it.

Be the same man in private that you are in public.
— Integrity is the alignment of what you say, what you
do, and who you are when no one is watching. The man
who is charming at dinner and cruel at home is not a
good man with a bad temper. He is a fraud. What you
do in the dark is who you actually are.

Stand up for the powerless. — The boy walks past
the injustice because it's not his problem. The man
stops. He speaks up for the man who can't speak for
himself. He stands between the bully and the target.
Not because it's convenient, but because it's right.
Silence in the presence of wrong is agreement with it.

Never stop growing. — The day you decide you've
arrived is the day you start dying. Read. Learn. Ask
questions. Listen to men wiser than you. Admit what
you don't know. A man who refuses to grow becomes a
man who takes up space without adding value. Growth
is not a phase of life. It is the point of life.

List 9: Ten Ways to Stop Performing and Start Being

**Delete the version of yourself you built for other
people.** — Somewhere along the way, you created a
character — the charming one, the tough one, the one
who always has it together. And that character became
so convincing that even you forgot it was a costume.
Take it off. The people who love you don't need your
highlight reel. They need you.

Stop posting your life and start living it. — The
moment you reach for the camera instead of being in

the moment, you've chosen the audience over the experience. Not everything needs to be documented, broadcast, or validated by strangers. The best parts of your life should be lived, not performed.

Say "I don't know" more often. — The performing man has an answer for everything because silence feels like weakness. The real man can sit in a conversation and admit he hasn't figured it out yet. "I don't know" is not a failure. It is a door — and on the other side of it is every truth you haven't yet discovered.

Let your wife see the mess. — She didn't marry a superhero. She married a man. And the man has doubts, fears, bad days, and questions he can't answer. If you hide those from her, you are not protecting her — you are isolating yourself. Intimacy is not possible without honesty. Let her in. She's stronger than you think.

Stop comparing your real life to another man's curated one. — The man you're envying online is not showing you his 2 a.m. arguments, his credit card debt, or the distance between him and his children. You are comparing your behind-the-scenes to his front stage. It's a rigged game. Quit playing it.

Do things no one will see. — Pray alone. Give anonymously. Clean up after yourself at a restaurant. Help the stranger. Do the right thing when there is zero chance of recognition. The man who only does good when someone is watching is not good. He is performing. Build a life of invisible integrity, and the visible stuff will take care of itself.

Let people be disappointed in you. — The performer rearranges his life to keep everyone happy. The real man understands that disappointing people is sometimes the cost of living with integrity. You cannot say yes to everything without saying no to yourself. And the man who says no when he needs to is the man who still has something left to give.

Sit with your failures instead of rebranding them. — The performer turns every failure into a lesson, every setback into a setup, every loss into a motivational speech. The real man can sit in the wreckage and say, "I failed. That hurt. And I'm not ready to spin it yet." Not everything needs a silver lining. Some things just need time.

Speak in your real voice. — Not the one you use at networking events. Not the one you use to impress your father-in-law. Not the one you use when you're trying to be the smartest man in the room. Your real voice — the one your wife hears at midnight when the walls come down. That's the voice the world needs. Use it more.

Measure your day by who you were, not what you produced. — Were you kind? Were you honest? Were you present? Did you look your children in the eye? Did you choose patience over reaction? The performer measures output. The man measures character. At the end of the day, no one standing at your grave is going to talk about your productivity.

List 10: Ten Ways to Carry Yourself with Quiet Confidence

Walk into a room like you belong there — because you do. — Not with arrogance. Not with apology. With the settled assurance of a man who knows that his worth is not determined by the room he's standing in. Shoulders back. Eyes forward. Not trying to be seen, but not trying to disappear. A man who carries himself well makes other people feel steady.

Make eye contact. — It's the simplest act of confidence there is. Look the person in the eye when you speak and when you listen. Not to dominate. Not to challenge. To connect. A man who can hold eye contact says, without words, "I see you, and I'm not afraid to be seen."

Speak less. Mean more. — Quiet confidence is not the absence of words. It's the discipline to choose them carefully. The man who talks constantly is often filling silence because he's afraid of it. The man who speaks with intention is the one people lean in to hear.

Dress like you respect yourself and the room. — This is not about fashion. It is about effort. A man who shows up wrinkled, unwashed, and careless is sending a message — that he doesn't think the moment, the people, or the occasion is worth his attention. You don't need expensive clothes. You need clean ones, ones that fit, and the discipline to put them on like a man who gives a damn.

Be the calmest person in the room during a crisis. — When everyone else is panicking, the man with quiet confidence becomes the anchor. He doesn't yell. He doesn't spiral. He assesses, speaks clearly, and acts. People follow calm. They always have. And the man who can be still when the world is shaking is the man everyone turns to.

Shake a man's hand like you mean it. — Firm. Brief. With eye contact. A handshake is a man's first and fastest introduction. It says more about you than your résumé, your title, or your shoes. Make it count.

Don't explain yourself to people who aren't asking. — The insecure man over-explains. He justifies, defends, and narrates every decision because he's afraid of being misunderstood. The confident man does what he does and lets the results speak. If someone wants to understand, they'll ask. And if they don't, that's fine too.

Give compliments freely and receive them gracefully. — A man with quiet confidence isn't threatened by another man's success. He can say, "That was impressive," without it costing him anything. And when someone compliments him, he doesn't deflect, deny, or downplay. He says, "Thank you." That's it. Deflecting praise is just insecurity wearing a humble mask.

Move with purpose. — Don't rush. Don't drag. Walk like a man who knows where he's going and isn't in a hurry to prove it. How a man moves tells the world whether he's anxious or anchored. Purpose in your step reflects purpose in your life. And people notice — even when they don't say so.

Be consistent. — Quiet confidence is not a moment. It's a pattern. The man who shows up the same way every day — steady, honest, prepared, kind — earns a trust that loud confidence never will. Anyone can be impressive once. The man who is reliably good, day after day, is the one people build their lives around.

MANHOOD & IDENTITY: QUOTES

"The ultimate measure of a man is not where he stands in moments of comfort and convenience, but where he stands at times of challenge and controversy." —Martin Luther King Jr.

"Nearly all men can stand adversity, but if you want to test a man's character, give him power." —Attributed to Abraham Lincoln

"A man who stands for nothing will fall for anything." —Malcolm X

"It is not the critic who counts; not the man who points out how the strong man stumbles, or where the doer of deeds could have done them better. The credit belongs to the man who is actually in the arena." —Theodore Roosevelt

"Watch your thoughts, for they become words. Watch your words, for they become actions. Watch your actions, for they become habits. Watch your habits, for they become character. Watch your character, for it becomes your destiny." —Attributed to Lao Tzu

"When I was a child, I talked like a child, I thought like a child, I reasoned like a child. When I became a man, I put the ways of childhood behind me." —1 Corinthians 13:11

"The world offers you comfort. But you were not made for comfort. You were made for greatness." — Attributed to Pope Benedict XVI

"Hard times create strong men. Strong men create good times. Good times create weak men. And weak men create hard times." —G. Michael Hopf

"He who conquers himself is the mightiest warrior." — Confucius

"As iron sharpens iron, so one person sharpens another." —Proverbs 27:17

MANHOOD & IDENTITY: PUTTING IT INTO PRACTICE

This week, write a personal creed. — In one page or less, define what you believe about manhood, faith, family, and purpose. Put it in your own words. Don't borrow someone else's language. This is your foundation. Read it once a week for the next month. Revise it as you grow.

Identify one mask you've been wearing — and take it off. — Choose one relationship where you've been performing instead of being real. This week, tell that person something honest that you've been holding back. Not to shock them. To let them know the real you. Start small. Start honest.

Spend one hour this week in complete silence — no screen, no sound. — Sit with yourself. Walk alone. Drive without noise. Let the thoughts come. Don't run from them. The man you are becoming cannot emerge from under the noise until you turn the noise off.

Find one man you trust and tell him one thing you've never told anyone. — Not on social media. In person or on a phone call. Something real. Something that costs you to say. Brotherhood doesn't begin with casual conversation. It begins with the courage to be known.

Evaluate your daily habits for one week. — Track how many hours you spend on a screen that isn't work. Track how many conversations you have face to face. Track how many times you reach for a device out of boredom. The data will tell you who's in charge — you or the machine.

Apologize to one person you've wronged and don't explain yourself. — No "but." No context. No justification. Just: "I was wrong. I'm sorry." The act of a clean apology is one of the most masculine things a man can do. It requires strength, humility, and the willingness to stand in the discomfort of accountability.

Set one boundary this week that you've been afraid to set. — With a friend, a coworker, a family member, or a habit. Say no to something that's been draining you. Not with anger. With clarity. Boundaries are not walls. They are the edges of a life that has been intentionally designed.

Read one chapter of Proverbs every day for the next month. — There are thirty-one chapters. One for each day. Proverbs was written for men who wanted wisdom more than wealth, character more than comfort. Read it slowly. Write down what hits you. Let it shape the way you think.

Turn off all notifications on your phone for one full day. — Not airplane mode. Just the notifications. See how many times you reach for it anyway. See how long it takes before the silence stops feeling like deprivation and starts feeling like freedom. The device is supposed to serve you — not summon you.

Ask your wife or your closest friend this question: "What's one thing I could do better?" — And listen to the answer. Don't defend. Don't deflect. Don't explain. Just receive it. The man who invites honest feedback is the man who never stops growing. And the man who never stops growing is the man who becomes worth following.

CATEGORY 2

BROTHERHOOD

List 1: Ten Ways to Build Friendships That Will Save Your Life

Stop waiting for someone to reach out first. — Most men are sitting alone in a room, hoping someone will call. And on the other side of town, another man is doing the same thing. The friendship you're starving for won't fall from the sky. Pick up the phone. Send the text. Show up at his door. The man who initiates is the man who builds — and building is always harder than waiting.

Find men who are going where you want to go. — You need friends who are building marriages, raising children, chasing purpose, and walking with God. Not because you're too good for anyone else, but because proximity shapes direction. You will become the average of the men you spend the most time with. Choose men who pull you forward, not men who make staying stuck feel comfortable.

Be willing to go beyond surface level. — "How's it going?" "Good." That's not friendship. That's a transaction. Real friendship starts when one man has the courage to say, "Actually, I'm not doing great," and the other man has the maturity to sit in it without trying to fix it. Most men have a dozen acquaintances and zero friends — because they've never gone deeper than the weather.

Show up in the hard seasons, not just the good ones. — Any man can be your friend at the barbecue. The one who shows up at the hospital, at the funeral, at 2 a.m. when your world is falling apart — that's your brother. And if you want that kind of friend, you have to be that kind of friend first. Friendship is not a spectator sport. It's boots on the ground.

Have a standing rhythm. — Friendships that survive are friendships that have structure. A weekly coffee. A monthly dinner. A Saturday morning walk. Not because the conversation is always deep, but because the consistency is. A man who shows up every Tuesday is a man who has said, without words, "You matter to me enough to keep coming back."

Tell the truth, even when it's uncomfortable. — A real friend will say the thing you don't want to hear. "You're drinking too much." "You're neglecting your wife." "You're making a mistake." Not to lecture — to love. The man who only tells you what you want to hear is not your friend. He's your audience. And audiences leave when the show gets boring.

Protect his reputation when he's not in the room. — If someone brings up your friend's name to tear it down, shut it down. Don't participate. Don't laugh along. Don't stay silent. A man who won't defend his brother's name behind his back doesn't deserve to stand beside him face to face.

Be the friend who remembers. — His wife's name. His daughter's birthday. The thing he's been struggling with. The goal he mentioned three months ago. Remembering is not a personality trait. It's a discipline. And it tells a man that you actually listened — that he wasn't just noise in your day, but someone worth paying attention to.

Don't keep score. — Real friendship is not a ledger. If you're counting who called last, who drove farther, who paid more — you're managing a transaction, not building a brotherhood. Give freely. Show up freely. And if there's a season where one man carries more weight, carry it without resentment. That's what brothers do.

Accept that real friendship takes years. — You don't build a foxhole bond over lunch. It takes shared meals, hard conversations, honest failures, late-night calls, and enough time for the masks to fall off. The men who will save your life are the men who have seen your worst and stayed. That doesn't happen in a month. It happens in a decade. Start now.

List 2: Ten Things a Real Friend Will Do That a Fake One Never Will

He will tell you the truth when the truth hurts. — A fake friend tells you what you want to hear because it keeps the peace. A real friend tells you what you need to hear because he cares more about your future than your feelings. The sting of an honest word from a brother is worth more than a thousand empty compliments from a man who doesn't have the guts to be straight with you.

He will show up when it's inconvenient. — A real friend doesn't check his calendar before deciding whether your crisis matters. He shows up — at midnight, on a workday, in the rain — because your pain is not an appointment to be scheduled. A fake friend sends a text that says, "Let me know if you need anything." A real friend is already at your door.

He will hold your secret like it's his own. — You told him something in confidence. Something that could embarrass you. Something that could cost you. And he will take it to his grave. A fake friend turns your vulnerability into a conversation starter at someone else's dinner table. A real friend treats your trust like it's sacred — because it is.

He will challenge your decisions without challenging your dignity. — "I think you're making a mistake" is not the same as "You're an idiot." A real friend can push back on your choices without belittling you. He pulls you aside. He speaks privately. He disagrees with your direction without disrespecting your person. A fake friend either says nothing or says it in front of everyone.

He will celebrate your wins without jealousy. — Your promotion. Your new house. Your marriage. A real friend is genuinely happy for you — not performing happiness while calculating how your success makes him feel smaller. Jealousy is the termite of friendship. It eats from the inside, and by the time you see the damage, the structure is gone.

He will mourn with you without rushing you. — A fake friend gives you a week to grieve and then starts dropping hints that you should be over it. A real friend sits in the grief with you — for as long as it takes — without a timeline or a motivational speech. He doesn't say, "Everything happens for a reason." He says, "I'm here. Take as long as you need."

He will call you out on your nonsense. — A real friend doesn't let you lie to yourself. If you're slipping — in your marriage, your faith, your habits, your character — he says something. Not because he enjoys the confrontation, but because he loves you too much to watch you fall apart in silence. A fake friend watches the train wreck and tells you everything's fine.

He will forgive you when you fail him. — You will let your friends down. It's not a possibility — it's a guarantee. The question is not whether you'll fail, but whether the friendship can survive it. A fake friend holds the grudge. A real friend says, "That hurt. But you're still my brother." And then he proves it by staying.

He will make time for you even when life gets full. — A real friend doesn't disappear when he gets married, has kids, gets promoted, or moves across the country. He adjusts, but he doesn't abandon. He calls. He visits. He makes it clear that the relationship matters, not by grand gestures, but by consistent small ones. Fake friends evaporate. Real friends endure.

He will pray for you without you asking. — Not as a performance. Not as a text that says, "Praying for you, bro." But actually praying — on his knees, in his car, in the quiet — asking God to cover you, protect you, guide you. A man who prays for his friend is a man who has taken the friendship beyond the human and into the eternal. And that kind of friend is worth more than gold.

List 3: Ten Ways to Be the Friend Every Man Needs but Few Have

Initiate, always. — Don't wait for the invitation. Be the man who calls first, who organizes the dinner, who reaches out on a Tuesday for no reason. Most men are lonely not because no one cares, but because no one makes the first move. Be the one who breaks the silence. Every time. Without keeping track.

Listen more than you advise. — Most men think being a good friend means having the right answer. It doesn't. It means having the right posture — leaned in, mouth closed, phone down. When a man opens up to you, the last thing he needs is a lecture. He needs to be heard. Give him the dignity of your full attention before you give him a single word of guidance.

Remember what matters to him. — His son's name. The surgery his wife had. The project at work he was nervous about. The conversation you had three weeks ago about his father. When you follow up on the details, you are saying, without words, "I was actually listening. You actually matter." That alone puts you in the top one percent of friendships most men have ever had.

Don't disappear when you get busy. — This is where most male friendships die — not in conflict, but in neglect. Life fills up. Jobs change. Kids come. And one day you realize you haven't talked to your closest friend in eight months. Don't let it happen. A five-minute phone call every other week is enough to keep a friendship alive. Silence is what kills it.

Be honest about your own struggles. — You cannot expect vulnerability from a man you refuse to be vulnerable with. If you want him to open up, open first. Tell him where you're weak. Tell him what you're fighting. Tell him what you're afraid of. The man who goes first sets the temperature for the entire friendship — and the temperature you set should be honesty.

Defend him to his face and behind his back. — When someone criticizes your friend in his absence, speak up. And when he's standing right in front of you questioning his own worth, speak up then, too. A good friend is a man who refuses to let his brother be torn apart — by others or by himself.

Show up with your hands, not just your words. — He's moving? Help him carry boxes. His car broke down? Drive across town. His wife is sick? Bring food. Friendship is not a text exchange. It's an action. And the men who show up with their hands are the men who build bonds that nothing can break.

Hold him accountable without holding it over his head. — You saw him slipping. You said something. He heard you. Now let it go. Don't bring it up every time you see him. Don't treat the thing he confessed as ammunition for the next disagreement. Accountability is a one-time conversation, not a permanent weapon. If you can't let it go after you've said it, you weren't holding him accountable — you were holding him hostage.

Celebrate him out loud. — Most men never hear another man say, "I'm proud of you." Not from a friend. Not from a father. Not from anyone. Be the man who says it. Tell your friend he's doing a good job. Tell him his family is better because of him. Tell him you see the work he's putting in. A single sentence of affirmation from a brother can carry a man through a season he wasn't sure he'd survive.

Stay when everyone else leaves. — There will come a season — maybe more than one — when your friend is not fun to be around. When he's angry, broken, depressed, difficult, or drowning. The fake friends will drift away. The acquaintances will stop calling. But you

— you stay. You sit in the wreckage with him. You don't try to fix it. You just refuse to leave. That's the friend every man needs. Be that.

List 4: Ten Ways to Have the Hard Conversation Instead of Walking Away

Say it in person, not on a screen. — Hard conversations do not belong in a text message. A screen gives you distance, but distance is exactly what a hard conversation doesn't need. Sit across from the man. Look him in the eye. Let him see your face when you say what needs to be said. The medium matters because it tells him whether you respect him enough to show up.

Start with what you value, not what you're angry about. — Before you deliver the hard truth, remind him why you're delivering it. "You matter to me. This friendship matters to me. That's why I'm saying this." When a man knows you're coming from love, he can hear things he'd never accept from anyone else. Lead with the relationship, not the grievance.

Use his name. — There is something about hearing your own name that disarms a man. It pulls him out of defense mode and into attention. "John, I need to talk to you about something." It's personal. It's direct. And it tells him you're not talking at him — you're talking to him.

Be specific, not vague. — "You've been different lately" helps no one. "The last three times we've been together, you've been on your phone the entire time" gives him something to work with. Vague concerns feel like attacks. Specific observations feel like invitations. Give the man something he can actually respond to.

Don't pile on. — One issue per conversation. If you've saved up six months of grievances and unload them all at once, you haven't had a hard conversation — you've had an ambush. Address the most important thing first. If there are others, they can wait. A man can absorb one truth at a time. He cannot absorb a list of indictments.

Let him respond without interrupting. — You said your piece. Now close your mouth and let him talk. He may get defensive. He may push back. He may say something that hurts. But if you don't give him the space to respond, you haven't had a conversation — you've delivered a verdict. And verdicts don't build friendships. Dialogue does.

Don't weaponize what he's told you in confidence. — The hard conversation should be about what you've observed, not what he confided. If he told you something vulnerable and you throw it back at him during a disagreement, you haven't been honest — you've been cruel. And he will never trust you again. Some ammunition is off-limits. Always.

Be prepared to hear something about yourself. — When you hold up a mirror, don't be surprised if someone holds one back. A man who confronts but can't be confronted is a man who's more interested in control than growth. If he has something to say about your behavior, hear it. The hard conversation goes both directions — or it doesn't go at all.

Don't leave without a path forward. — The goal is not to make your point. The goal is to make things better. Before you walk away, establish what comes next. "I want us to be straight with each other." "Can we try this differently?" "Let's check in next week." A hard conversation without a path forward is just a wound without a bandage.

Follow up. — The conversation doesn't end when you stand up. Check in a week later. Not to police him — to show him that the relationship survived the tension. A text that says, "Hey, I'm glad we talked. You good?" tells a man that the hard thing didn't break anything. And that makes the next hard conversation possible instead of impossible.

List 5: Ten Ways to Show Up for Another Man Without Being Asked

Bring food when his world falls apart. — When a man's wife is sick, when he loses a parent, when his child is in the hospital — don't ask what he needs. Bring a meal. Bring it to the door. Don't make him host you. Don't make him talk. Just hand it to him and say, "I'm here if you need me." That one act will matter more than a hundred text messages.

Mow his lawn when he can't. — When he's traveling for work, recovering from surgery, or going through something that has him on his knees — show up with a mower. Don't tell him. Just do it. A man who serves without announcement is a man who understands that love is not a performance. It's a verb.

Sit with him in the waiting room. — When the diagnosis is bad, when the surgery is long, when the test results haven't come back — be the man in the chair beside him. You don't need to have the right words. You don't need to fix anything. You just need to not let him sit there alone. Presence is the most undervalued gift one man can give another.

Call him on the anniversary of his loss. — Everyone shows up in the first week. Almost no one remembers the one-year mark. The day his father died. The day his marriage ended. The day his child was buried. Mark it in your calendar. Call him. He won't expect it. And that's exactly why it will matter. Grief doesn't end when the casseroles stop coming. It just gets lonelier.

Cover his shift. — At work. At church. In the carpool rotation. Wherever a man is stretched thin, step in and take something off his plate without being asked. Don't say, "Let me know if you need help." That puts the burden on him to ask. Say, "I'm handling Thursday. It's done." That's not an offer. That's a brother.

Notice when he's withdrawing. — Men don't announce when they're drowning. They get quieter. They cancel plans. They stop calling. They stare at their screens longer than they should. If your friend is pulling away, don't wait for him to come back. Go to him. Knock on the door — literally or figuratively. A man who disappears without anyone noticing is a man who has learned that no one is paying attention. Prove him wrong.

Walk with him when he's making a big decision. — Not to tell him what to do. To help him think out loud.

To ask the questions he's too close to see. "What does your wife think?" "What happens if it doesn't work?" "What are you afraid of?" The man who walks alongside another man's decision-making process is the man who gets invited into the decisions that actually matter.

Send the message you're thinking but wouldn't normally send. — "I was thinking about you today." "I'm proud of who you're becoming." "You've been a better friend to me than I probably deserve." Most men have these thoughts and never say them. They feel awkward, unnecessary, too soft. Send it anyway. The man on the other end of that message may be reading it at the exact moment he needed to hear it.

Invite him in before he has to ask. — To the table. To the trip. To the group. Many men are standing on the outside of friendships they desperately want to be a part of, waiting for permission to enter. Be the man who opens the door. Pull up a chair. Make room. A simple "You should come with us" can change the trajectory of a man's isolation.

Pray for him — and tell him you are. — Not in a public, performative way. Privately. Then tell him. "Hey, I've been praying for you this week." That sentence carries a weight most men don't realize until they hear it. It says, "I thought about you when I didn't have to. And I brought you before God because I believe He listens." There is no greater act of brotherhood.

List 6: Ten Ways to Hold Another Man Accountable Without Destroying the Relationship

Earn the right before you speak. — You cannot hold a man accountable if you haven't first invested in him. If you haven't been to his house, met his family, sat with him in his pain, and proven that you're in his corner — your correction will feel like judgment, not love. Relationship is the currency that buys you the right to speak hard truth. Earn it first.

Ask permission to go there. — Before you deliver the blow, ask. "Can I be straight with you about something?" That one sentence changes the entire posture of the conversation. It invites instead of ambushes. It gives him the dignity of choosing to listen rather than being forced to hear. Most men will say yes — and the fact that you asked will make the truth land softer.

Speak to the behavior, not the character. — "What you did was reckless" is very different from "You're a reckless person." One names the action. The other names the man. When you attack his character, he will defend it — and the conversation is over. When you address the behavior, he can own it without feeling like his entire identity is on trial.

Be specific about what you saw. — "I noticed you've been drinking every night this week." "I heard how you spoke to your wife at dinner." "You've canceled on us three times in a row." Give him facts, not feelings. Specific observations create space for honest conversation. General accusations create walls.

Don't do it in front of other people. — Accountability is a private act. If you confront a man in front of his wife, his friends, his coworkers, or his children, you haven't held him accountable — you've humiliated him. And humiliation does not produce change. It produces resentment, shame, and distance. Pull him aside. Close the door. Keep it between brothers.

Be prepared for pushback — and don't crumble. — He might deny it. He might get angry. He might turn it back on you. That doesn't mean you were wrong to say it. It means the truth is doing its work, and the work is uncomfortable. Stand your ground gently. Don't escalate. Don't back down. Let the truth sit in the room and breathe.

Make it clear that the relationship is not at risk. — "I'm not going anywhere. I'm saying this because I care about you too much to watch this happen in silence." That sentence is the difference between accountability and abandonment. A man who hears correction from someone he knows will stay is a man who can actually receive it.

Check your own hands first. — Before you point at another man's sin, examine your own. Not because you have to be perfect to speak truth — you don't — but because a man can smell hypocrisy from across the room. If you're calling out his anger while your own house is full of it, your words carry no weight. Clean your own hands before you reach for his.

Follow up with presence, not pressure. — After the conversation, don't disappear. And don't hover. Show up the same way you always have — with a text, a call, a shared meal. Let the conversation settle. Don't bring it up again unless he does or unless the behavior continues. The goal is not to monitor him. The goal is to love him well enough that he monitors himself.

Accept that it might cost you. — Some men will not hear it. Some men will walk away. Some friendships will not survive the truth. And that is a grief worth mourning — but it is not a reason to stay silent. A man who withholds truth to preserve a friendship has chosen comfort over love. And love, real love, tells the truth even when it costs everything.

List 7: Ten Ways to Forgive a Brother Who Let You Down

Name what he did — clearly and honestly. — You cannot forgive something you haven't fully acknowledged. Don't minimize it. Don't pretend it didn't happen. Don't spiritualize it away. He broke your trust. He wasn't there when you needed him. He said something behind your back. Name it. Feel it. Only then can you begin to release it.

Separate the wound from the man. — What he did hurt you. But what he did is not all he is. The man who let you down is the same man who showed up a hundred times before. The same man who answered the phone at midnight. The same man who carried your burden when it was too heavy. One failure does not erase an entire friendship — unless you let it.

Decide whether this is a pattern or a moment. — There is a difference between a man who stumbled and a man who makes stumbling his way of life. If this was a one-time failure, extend grace. If it's the tenth time he's done the same thing, the conversation changes. Forgiveness doesn't require you to keep walking into the same wall. Sometimes it means forgiving him and walking a different direction.

Stop rehearsing the offense. — Every time you replay the moment — in your head, in your conversations, in your prayers — you are re-injuring yourself. Bitterness is a wound that you reopen every time you revisit the story. At some point, you have to close the file. Not because what he did was acceptable, but because the replay is doing more damage than the original act.

Say it out loud — to him. — Forgiveness that stays in your head is incomplete. At some point, if the relationship matters, sit across from him and say, "What you did hurt me. I've struggled with it. But I forgive you. I want to move forward." That sentence is not for him. It is for both of you. It clears the air and reopens the door.

Don't use the failure as leverage. — Once you forgive, it's off the table. You don't get to bring it up in the next argument. You don't get to hold it over his head when you need a tactical advantage. Forgiveness with conditions is not forgiveness — it's a loan. And loans collect interest. Let it go completely, or admit you haven't forgiven yet. Both are honest. Only one sets you free.

Grieve what the friendship lost. — Some things don't go back to the way they were. The trust may be rebuilt, but it will be rebuilt differently. And that's okay. Grieve the version of the friendship that existed before the failure, and be open to the version that comes after. It may be deeper. It may be more honest. It may be stronger for having survived the break.

Remember your own failures. — You have let people down. You have broken trust. You have failed to show up. And someone — a wife, a friend, a parent, a God — extended you grace you did not deserve. That memory should make forgiveness not just possible, but natural. The man who has been forgiven much should be the first to forgive.

Pray for him. — Not the passive kind. The real kind. Ask God to bless him. Ask God to protect his family. Ask God to grow him into the man he's supposed to become. It is almost impossible to remain bitter toward a man you are genuinely praying for. Prayer doesn't just change the other person. It changes you.

Give the friendship time to heal. — Forgiveness is a decision. Healing is a process. Don't rush it. Don't pretend everything is fine when it's not. Let the friendship breathe. Let the trust rebuild slowly, one conversation at a time, one kept promise at a time. The strongest friendships in the world are not the ones that were never broken. They are the ones that survived the break.

List 8: Ten Ways to Build a Circle That Sharpens You

Be intentional about who sits at your table. — Your inner circle should not be assembled by accident. Choose men who challenge you, not just men who agree with you. Choose men who are building something, not just consuming. Choose men whose lives you want to learn from, not just men who make you feel comfortable. Comfort is not the goal. Growth is.

Keep the circle small. — You don't need a dozen close friends. You need three to five men who know the real you. Men you would call at 2 a.m. Men who have seen you at your worst and didn't leave. A large network is useful for business. A small circle is essential for survival. Don't confuse the two.

Include men who are ahead of you. — You need at least one man in your life who has already walked the road you're on. A man who has been married longer, fathered longer, led longer, suffered longer. Not a guru — a guide. Someone who can say, "I've been there. Here's what I learned." Humility is the price of admission. Pay it gladly.

Include men who are behind you. — You also need men who are watching you, learning from you, looking to you for the example you're setting. Mentoring another man forces you to live what you teach. It sharpens your discipline because someone else is depending on it. The man who only receives from older men but never gives to younger men has broken the chain.

Set the standard for honesty. — If your circle is full of surface-level conversations, it's because someone set that standard — and it might have been you. Go first. Be the man who says, "I've been struggling with this." Be the man who admits failure. Be the man who asks the uncomfortable question. The circle takes its cues from the bravest man in it. Make sure that's you.

Meet regularly and consistently. — A brotherhood that meets when it's convenient will never survive when it's not. Set a schedule. Weekly. Biweekly. Monthly at the bare minimum. Guard it the way you guard your work meetings. Cancel your convenience, not your brotherhood. The men who show up consistently are the men who will be there when showing up costs something.

Make the time screen-free. — When you're together, put the devices away. All of them. Eye contact. Real voices. Undivided attention. The quality of your brotherhood is directly proportional to the amount of attention you give it. A man who scrolls through his phone while his brother is talking is a man who has already decided the relationship isn't worth his full presence.

Don't let one man dominate. — A good circle has shared airtime. If the same man talks every week while the others listen, the circle has become a performance, not a partnership. Create space for the quiet man to speak. Ask direct questions. Draw out the ones who hold back. The man who says the least may be carrying the most.

Hold each other accountable by agreement. —
Don't assume the role of accountability. Establish it.
Say, "I want you to ask me about this every week." Give
each other specific areas to check in on — anger,
drinking, screen use, presence with family.
Accountability works best when it's invited, not
imposed. And when every man in the circle is both
giving and receiving it.

Protect what's shared in the circle. — What's said in
the room stays in the room. No exceptions. If a man
confesses something vulnerable and it shows up in
conversation outside the group, the circle is dead.
Confidentiality is not a suggestion. It is the foundation.
Without it, no man will ever risk being honest. And
without honesty, the circle has no purpose.

List 9: Ten Ways to Be Vulnerable Without Losing Respect

**Understand that vulnerability is not weakness —
it's warfare.** — The easiest thing in the world is to
hide. To perform. To keep the mask on and let everyone
believe you've got it together. Vulnerability is the
harder path. It requires you to stand in front of another
person unarmed, without pretense, and say, "This is
who I am." That's not weakness. That's the kind of
courage most men never find.

Choose the right audience. — Vulnerability is not a
broadcast. It is a conversation. Don't bare your soul on
the internet, at a dinner party, or to a man you met last
month. Choose the man who has proven his

trustworthiness over time. Choose the wife who has stayed through the hard seasons. The wrong audience will use your vulnerability against you. The right one will hold it like gold.

Start with something small. — You don't have to begin with your deepest wound. Start with an honest admission. "I've been anxious about this." "I haven't been sleeping well." "I'm not sure I'm doing this right." Small honesty opens the door for larger honesty later. And each step builds the trust that makes the bigger revelations possible.

Don't confuse vulnerability with venting. — Venting is dumping your frustration on another person without accountability. Vulnerability is owning your role in the mess. "I'm angry and I've been taking it out on my family" is vulnerable. "Everyone is making my life miserable" is venting. One leads to growth. The other leads to more of the same.

Say what you're actually feeling, not what sounds acceptable. — "I'm fine" is the most common lie men tell. Replace it with the truth. "I'm overwhelmed." "I'm scared." "I don't know how to do this." Those words feel dangerous because the world taught you that admitting them makes you less of a man. The opposite is true. The man who can name his feelings is the man who won't be controlled by them.

Don't apologize for being human. — You don't have to preface your honesty with, "Sorry, I know this is a lot." You don't have to perform shame about having needs, fears, or doubts. Every man has them. The ones who admit it are not the weakest in the room — they are the bravest. Stop apologizing for needing what every human being needs: to be known and not rejected.

Let your wife see you struggle. — Too many men treat their marriage like a job performance review. They manage their image. They curate their strength. And their wife sleeps beside a man she doesn't actually know. Let her see the doubt. Let her see the fear. Let her see the man behind the provider. She didn't marry a résumé. She married a person. Give her access to him.

Accept that some men won't understand. — When you're vulnerable, not every man will respond well. Some will get uncomfortable. Some will change the subject. Some will joke to deflect. That's their issue, not yours. Don't let one man's discomfort stop you from being honest with another. The ones who can handle it are the ones worth building with.

Be vulnerable about your victories, too. — Vulnerability is not just about pain. It's also about admitting what you're proud of, what you hope for, what you're dreaming about. Men are often more afraid to say, "I want this so badly I can taste it" than they are to say, "I'm falling apart." Both take courage. Share both.

Remember that vulnerability deepens respect — it doesn't diminish it. — The man who tells the truth about his struggles and keeps showing up anyway is the man other men want to follow. Not the man who pretends he never bleeds. Not the man who performs invincibility. The man who stands up, admits the wound, and walks forward anyway. That man doesn't lose respect. He earns it — the kind that can't be faked.

List 10: Ten Ways to Recognize When You're Isolated and What to Do About It

You can't name one man who truly knows you. — Not a coworker. Not a neighbor. Not a man from church you exchange pleasantries with on Sunday. A man who knows what you're carrying. A man who knows about the argument you had last night, the fear that keeps you up at 3 a.m., the thing you've been hiding for years. If no name comes to mind, you're isolated.

Your phone is your primary companion. — When the first thing you reach for in the morning and the last thing you hold at night is a screen — and the time in between is filled with scrolling, swiping, and consuming instead of connecting — you have replaced community with content. Content doesn't call you by name. Content doesn't show up at the hospital. Content doesn't grieve with you. It numbs you. And numb is not the same as known.

You haven't had a real conversation in weeks. — Not about the weather. Not about the game. A real conversation — the kind where someone asks how you're actually doing and you tell the truth. If weeks have passed without one, you are not just busy. You are drifting. And drifting always ends in the same place: alone.

You've stopped being honest about how you're doing. — When every answer is "fine" or "good" or "can't complain," and none of them are true — that's isolation wearing a social mask. You're surrounded by people but known by none of them. And the gap between your public self and your private reality is growing wider every day.

You feel relief when plans get canceled. — There's a difference between needing rest and hiding from people. If the predominant feeling when someone cancels on you is relief, something has shifted. You've started building walls where bridges used to be. And walls, once built, are hard to take down — especially when you've convinced yourself they're for your protection.

You've been keeping a secret that's eating you alive. — Every isolated man is carrying something he hasn't told anyone. An addiction. A failure. A fear. A sin. And the longer he carries it alone, the heavier it gets — and the more convinced he becomes that telling someone will destroy him. It won't. The secret is what's destroying you. Sunlight is the cure.

Start with one phone call. — You don't have to rebuild a social life overnight. Call one man. One. Say, "Hey, I realized we haven't talked in a while. Can we grab coffee?" That's it. One small act of reaching out. The hardest part is the first move — and the first move doesn't have to be dramatic. It just has to be real.

Tell someone the truth. — Find a man you trust — or a man you used to trust — and tell him what you've been carrying. "I've been struggling." "I've been alone." "I don't know how to ask for help." You don't need a polished confession. You need a raw one. And the man who receives it with grace will be the man who walks you out of the dark.

Join something. — A small group. A men's Bible study. A gym. A service project. A breakfast table at a diner every Thursday morning. Put yourself in a room with other men on a regular basis. Friendship doesn't happen in isolation — it happens in proximity. And proximity requires you to show up somewhere, consistently, even when you don't feel like it.

Stop telling yourself you don't need anyone. — That's the oldest lie isolation tells. It whispers that independence is strength and needing people is weakness. It's wrong. Every great man in history had men around him — counselors, brothers, friends who held him up when he couldn't stand. You are no different. You need other men. Admitting it is not defeat. It is the beginning of everything that matters.

BROTHERHOOD: QUOTES

"As iron sharpens iron, so one man sharpens another." —Proverbs 27:17

"Faithful are the wounds of a friend; profuse are the kisses of an enemy." —Proverbs 27:6

"Two are better than one, because they have a good return for their labor: If either of them falls down, one can help the other up. But pity anyone who falls and has no one to help them up." —Ecclesiastes 4:9-10

"A friend loves at all times, and a brother is born for a time of adversity." —Proverbs 17:17

"The glory of friendship is not the outstretched hand, not the kindly smile, nor the joy of companionship; it is the spiritual inspiration that comes to one when you discover that someone else believes in you and is willing to trust you with a friendship." —Ralph Waldo Emerson

"No man is a failure who has friends." —Clarence, *It's a Wonderful Life*

"Greater love has no one than this: to lay down one's life for one's friends." —John 15:13

"The loneliest moment in someone's life is when they are watching their whole world fall apart, and all they can do is stare blankly." —F. Scott Fitzgerald

"I would rather walk with a friend in the dark, than alone in the light." —Helen Keller

"One loyal friend is worth ten thousand relatives." — Euripides

BROTHERHOOD: PUTTING IT INTO PRACTICE

Call one man this week and ask him how he's really doing. — Not a text. A phone call. Use his name. Ask the question and then be quiet. Let him answer. If he says, "I'm fine," ask again. "No, really — how are you?" That second ask is the one that opens the door.

Identify three men you want in your inner circle and tell them. — Say it directly: "I want us to be closer. I want to be the kind of friends who actually know each other." It will feel awkward. Do it anyway. The friendship you want on the other side of that conversation is worth the discomfort of starting it.

Schedule a recurring time with at least one friend. — Put it on the calendar. A weekly walk. A biweekly coffee. A monthly dinner. Treat it like a meeting that can't be canceled. Consistency is the foundation of brotherhood, and without a calendar, consistency dies.

Put your phone in another room the next time you're with a friend. — Give him your undivided attention for one full hour. No glances at notifications. No scrolling during silence. One hour of full presence. If that feels hard, it's because the screen has trained you to be somewhere else even when you're right here.

Send one honest text to a friend today. — Not "hey" or a meme. Something real. "I've been thinking about you." "You've been a good friend to me." "I'm going through something and I wanted you to know." One honest sentence. That's all it takes to crack open a door that's been closed for too long.

Confess one struggle to a man you trust. — Not publicly. Privately. In person if possible. Tell him the thing you've been carrying alone. Not for advice. For relief. The weight of a secret carried alone doubles every month. The weight of a secret shared with a brother is cut in half overnight.

Write down the names of five men who matter to you — and reach out to each one this month. — A call, a visit, a meal. Not all at once — one per week. Re-engage the friendships you've let fall silent. Most of them are not dead. They're just dormant. And dormant friendships can be awakened with a single act of intention.

Ask a friend to hold you accountable in one specific area. — Not a vague "keep me in check." A specific ask. "Ask me every week if I've been on my phone after 9 p.m." "Ask me how I spoke to my wife this week." "Ask me if I've been drinking alone." Invite the accountability. Make it precise. And don't get defensive when he follows through.

Apologize to a man you've failed. — You know who he is. You ghosted him. You didn't show up. You talked behind his back. You let the friendship die by neglect. Pick up the phone and own it. "I should have been a better friend. I'm sorry." Whether he accepts it or not, you'll be free. And he'll know that someone noticed the gap.

Pray for your friends by name every day this week. — Not a blanket "bless my friends" prayer. Say their names. Pray for their marriages. Their children. Their struggles. Their faith. When you pray for a man by name, he moves from the periphery of your life to the center. And the men at the center of your prayer life will become the men at the center of your actual life.

CATEGORY 3

FATHERHOOD

List 1: Ten Things Your Children Need from You More Than Money

Your presence at the table. — Not your body in the chair while your mind is somewhere else. Not the back of your phone held up like a wall between you and the people who love you most. Your presence — eyes on them, voice engaged, fully there. A child who eats dinner with a father who is actually in the room learns something no tutor, no gift, and no vacation can teach: that they are worth someone's undivided attention.

Your attention when they're talking. — A child who speaks to a father who doesn't look up is learning a lesson you didn't intend to teach — that they are interruptible, that they rank below whatever is on your screen, that their voice is not worth your time. Stop what you are doing. Kneel down. Look them in the eye. What they're telling you may sound small to you. To them, it is everything.

Your patience when they fail. — They will spill things, break things, forget things, and disappoint you. That's not disobedience — that's childhood. A father who explodes at every mistake raises a child who is afraid to try. A father who breathes, corrects gently, and offers a second chance raises a child who learns that failure is not fatal and that the man they trust most in the world has room for them to be imperfect.

Your words when they're doubting themselves. — "I believe in you." "I'm proud of you." "You can do this." A child who hears those words from their father carries them like armor into every hard thing they face. And a child who never hears them spends the rest of their life looking for someone — anyone — to say what their father never did. You have no idea how much power sits in your mouth. Use it to build them.

Your consistency. — Not perfection. Consistency. Showing up to the games, the recitals, the bedtimes, the breakfasts — not every single one, but enough that your children never have to wonder whether you'll be there. A father who is sometimes brilliant and often absent is a father who teaches his children that love is unreliable. Be steady. That's what they need. Not fireworks. Faithfulness.

Your apology when you're wrong. — A father who never says "I'm sorry" raises children who believe that power means never having to admit fault. A father who looks his child in the eye and says, "I was wrong. I shouldn't have said that. Will you forgive me?" raises children who understand that real strength includes humility. Your apology doesn't weaken your authority. It deepens their respect.

Your affection. — Hold them. Hug them. Kiss their foreheads. Roughhouse on the living room floor. Tell them you love them — out loud, with your voice, every single day. A child who is starved for a father's affection will search for it in every relationship they enter for the rest of their lives. And they will accept counterfeits because they never knew what the real thing felt like. Don't let that happen.

Your protection from things they're not ready for. — The world is not waiting for your children to grow up before it comes for them. Content they should never see is one unlocked screen away. Conversations they're not ready for are happening in every hallway. A father's job is not to shelter them from reality forever — it's to stand between them and the darkness until they're strong enough to face it. That's not overprotection. That's fatherhood.

Your example. — They are watching you. Every day. How you treat their mother. How you handle your anger. How you respond to disappointment. Whether you keep your promises. Whether you pray. Whether you serve. Whether you tell the truth. Your children will not remember most of what you said. They will remember everything you did. Live accordingly.

Your time. — Not your leftover time. Not the scraps between meetings and obligations. Your best time. The hours when you're most alive, most energetic, most yourself. Give those to your children — not to your inbox. One day the inbox will forget you ever existed. Your children never will. And what they remember will be shaped entirely by whether you gave them your time or your excuses.

List 2: Ten Ways to Raise a Son Who Becomes a Good Man

Let him see you love his mother. — A boy who watches his father honor, serve, and adore his wife learns how to treat a woman long before he ever dates one. He learns it in the kitchen when you wash the dishes. He learns it in the hallway when you hold her hand. He learns it in the argument when you lower your voice instead of raising it. You are writing his playbook. Make it one worth following.

Teach him to lose with dignity. — He will lose. At sports, at school, at friendships, at things he cared about deeply. The question is not whether he'll lose — it's how. Teach him to shake the other man's hand. Teach him to walk off the field without excuses. Teach him that losing well is a sign of character, and that the man who can lose without bitterness will eventually win at things that matter far more than games.

Let him struggle before you rescue him. — Every instinct in you will want to solve it for him. Don't. Let him carry the heavy thing. Let him figure out the problem. Let him sit in the discomfort of not knowing the answer. The muscles that will carry him through manhood — resilience, problem-solving, perseverance — are built in the moments you step back and let him fight.

Give him responsibility and hold him to it. — Chores. Commitments. Tasks that are his and his alone. Not because you need help around the house, but because a boy who learns to own a responsibility learns to own his life. Follow through matters. If he says he'll do it, hold him to it. A man's reliability is forged in boyhood — one kept promise at a time.

Teach him what real strength looks like. — Not the kind on the screen — the flexing, the shouting, the domination. The kind that sits quietly beside a grieving friend. The kind that apologizes when it's wrong. The kind that picks up the smaller kid who fell down and doesn't post about it. Tell your son, over and over, that the strongest men in the world are the ones who are gentle with the people around them.

Talk to him about the things no one else will. — Sex. Pornography. Alcohol. The pressure to perform. The loneliness that no boy wants to admit. If you don't have these conversations, the internet will — and it will lie to him about every single one. You don't have to have all the answers. You just have to be the man who isn't afraid to sit in the awkward and say, "Let's talk about this."

Let him see you fail — and recover. — If your son thinks you've never struggled, he'll believe that struggle means something is wrong with him. Let him see the missed shot, the lost job, the apology you had to make. More importantly, let him see what you did next. How you got back up. How you kept going. The lesson is not in the fall. It's in the rising.

Hold him accountable without shaming him. — There is a canyon-wide difference between, "What you did was wrong, and here's what we're going to do about it," and "What is wrong with you?" One corrects behavior. The other attacks identity. A boy who is shamed by his father doesn't learn discipline. He learns that he is fundamentally broken. Correct the action. Protect the boy.

Require him to look people in the eye and shake their hand. — This is not about etiquette. It is about character. A boy who can look another person in the eye and offer a firm handshake is a boy who is learning to be present, to be respectful, and to be unafraid. It starts at five years old and it carries him through every interview, every relationship, and every moment of leadership he'll ever face.

Tell him who he is before the world tells him who he should be. — "You are brave. You are kind. You are capable. You are loved." Say it to him so many times that by the time the world tries to hand him a counterfeit identity, he already has one that fits. A boy who knows who he is — because his father told him — is a boy the world cannot easily break.

List 3: Ten Ways to Raise a Daughter Who Knows Her Worth

Be the standard she measures every man against. — Whether you like it or not, you are her first definition of what a man is supposed to be. If you are kind, she will expect kindness. If you are faithful, she will expect faithfulness. If you are absent, dismissive, or cruel — she will expect that, too, and she will mistake it for normal. You are not just raising a daughter. You are shaping every relationship she'll ever have with a man.

Tell her she's beautiful — and tell her it's not the most important thing about her. — She will hear from the world, every single day, that her value is in her appearance. Counteract it. Tell her she's beautiful because she is. Then tell her she's smart. Tell her she's brave. Tell her she's kind. Tell her she's strong. Give her so many words for what she is that "beautiful" becomes just one of many — not the only one she clings to.

Listen to her without fixing. — When she comes to you with a problem, your instinct will be to solve it. Resist. Sometimes she doesn't need a solution. She needs a father who listens, who takes her seriously, who doesn't minimize what she's feeling. When you listen without jumping to the answer, you teach her that her voice matters — that she is worth being heard.

Set boundaries and hold them. — She will push. She will test. She will say you're being unfair. Hold the line anyway. A father who sets boundaries is not a father who is controlling — he is a father who is communicating that she is valuable enough to protect. The girl who grows up with clear, loving boundaries becomes the woman who knows how to set her own.

Apologize to her when you mess up. — She needs to know that men can be wrong and own it. That strength is not the absence of failure but the willingness to face it. When you look your daughter in the eye and say, "I was wrong, and I'm sorry," you are teaching her never to accept a man who can't do the same.

Let her see you serve. — Wash the dishes. Cook the meal. Fold the laundry. Do it without being asked and without complaint. When your daughter sees her father serve the household — not because he has to, but because he chooses to — she learns that service is not beneath a strong man. And she will never settle for a man who believes it is.

Take her on dates. — Not expensive ones. Intentional ones. A donut shop on Saturday morning. A walk around the block. Breakfast before school. The point is not the activity. The point is the attention — dedicated, undivided, just for her. A daughter who has been dated by her father knows what it feels like when a man makes her a priority. And she won't accept less.

Don't let the screen raise her. — The world is reaching your daughter through every device in your house. It is telling her what to wear, what to weigh, what to want, who to be. If you're not actively countering that message with your own voice, your own values, your own presence — the screen wins. And the screen does not love her.

Be present in her hard seasons. — She will go through things you don't understand — friendship drama, body image struggles, heartbreak, anxiety, pressure you can't see. Don't dismiss it because it doesn't look like your version of hard. It's hard to her. And a father who stays close during the storms she can't explain is a father who builds a trust that lasts decades.

Never stop showing up. — When she's five, she'll want you at every game. When she's fifteen, she might act like she doesn't. Show up anyway. When she's twenty-five, she'll remember every time you were there — and every time you weren't. A father who shows up consistently is a father who teaches his daughter the most important lesson she'll ever learn about men: the good ones don't leave.

List 4: Ten Ways to Discipline Without Destroying

Never discipline in anger. — If you're angry, you're not ready. Walk away. Breathe. Come back when you can see clearly. A father who disciplines in anger is not correcting his child — he is punishing them for how they made him feel. And a child who is disciplined by an angry man doesn't learn the lesson. They learn to fear the teacher.

Make the consequence fit the offense. — A child who forgets to clean his room does not need the same response as a child who lied to your face. Proportional discipline teaches discernment — it shows your child that not everything carries the same weight and that you see the difference between carelessness and defiance.

Explain the why. — "Because I said so" works when they're three. It fails when they're thirteen. A child who understands the reason behind the boundary respects it far more than a child who only fears the penalty. "I'm taking this away because you broke a commitment, and I'm teaching you that commitments matter." That's discipline that educates, not just punishes.

Separate the behavior from the child. — "What you did was wrong" is discipline. "You are a bad kid" is destruction. A child can recover from correction. A child who believes they are fundamentally bad —

because their father said so — will spend years trying to outrun an identity they never should have been given.

Be consistent between parents. — If you say no and their mother says yes — or the other way around — the child learns to play the gap. Discipline requires a united front. Talk to your wife. Agree on the standard. Present it together. A house divided on discipline is a house where the child has already won — and winning without boundaries is losing in the long run.

Follow through every time. — If you say, "If you do that again, this happens," then it must happen. A father who threatens without following through teaches his child that words don't mean anything — including words like "I love you" and "I'm proud of you." Your word is either reliable or it isn't. There is no middle ground.

Discipline privately, not publicly. — Do not correct your child in front of their friends, their siblings, or a room full of strangers. Pull them aside. Close the door. Have the conversation where their dignity is intact. A child who is humiliated publicly does not learn respect. They learn shame. And shame doesn't correct behavior — it buries it.

Restore the relationship immediately after. — The discipline is the correction. The restoration is the point. After the consequence, hold them. Tell them you love them. Tell them the discipline doesn't change how you feel about them. A child who is disciplined and then embraced learns that correction is an act of love, not rejection. A child who is disciplined and then ignored learns that love is conditional.

Ask yourself whose frustration you're really addressing. — Sometimes the discipline is really about your day, your stress, your exhaustion. The child's offense is small, but your fuse is shorter than it should be. Before you correct, pause and ask: is this about what they did, or about how I feel? If it's the latter, the correction can wait until you've dealt with yourself first.

Model what you're asking them to become. — You cannot demand honesty while you lie. You cannot demand patience while you explode. You cannot demand kindness while you tear people apart at the dinner table. Discipline without example is hypocrisy — and children can smell hypocrisy before they can spell it. Be the standard before you enforce it.

List 5: Ten Ways to Stay Present When Your Work Demands Everything

Decide before you walk through the door. — On the drive home, in the elevator, in the driveway — make a conscious decision to transition. Work is behind you. Your family is ahead of you. You cannot carry both at the same time. Choose. The emails will be there in the morning. Your daughter's story about her day will not.

Put the device in a drawer from dinner to bedtime. — Not on silent. Not face down. In a drawer. If it's in your hand, it wins. If it's in your pocket, it's calling. If it's in a drawer, you're free. Two hours.

That's all. Two hours of being fully present with the people who will remember you long after your employer forgets your name.

Protect one sacred time and never negotiate it. — Bedtime stories. Saturday morning breakfast. Sunday afternoon. Pick one and wall it off like it's the most important meeting of your week — because it is. Your children will not remember your quarterly reports. They will remember the thing you always did with them. Give them something to remember.

Learn to say no to the things that steal from your family. — The extra project. The weekend obligation. The dinner with colleagues that could be an email. Every yes to work is a no to someone at home. That math doesn't change just because the work feels important. Count the cost before you answer.

Stop checking in. Start checking out. — If you're at the dinner table reading emails under the table, you're not present — you're performing presence. Your family can tell the difference. Checking out of work is not laziness. It is a discipline. It is the decision that the people in this room deserve the same focus you give your clients.

Talk to your children about your work — simply and honestly. — They don't need the details. They need to know that what you do matters, that you do it with integrity, and that you come home to them because they matter more. "Daddy had a hard day, but I'm glad to be here with you" teaches a child more about work and priorities than any lecture ever could.

Schedule your family before you schedule your work. — Most men fill their calendar with work obligations first and then try to squeeze their family into the gaps. Reverse it. Block the game. Block the recital. Block the family dinner. Then build work around it. The things on your calendar reveal your real priorities. Make sure your family isn't an afterthought.

Be honest when you're struggling to be present. — Your wife sees it. Your kids feel it. Instead of pretending, say it out loud. "I'm having a hard time shutting my brain off tonight. I'm going to take ten minutes and then I'm all yours." Honesty buys grace. Pretending buys resentment.

Remember that no one on their deathbed wishes they'd worked more. — They wish they'd been there for the first steps. The last game. The night she needed to talk. The morning he wanted to show you something. Work is necessary. Work can be meaningful. But work will never hold your hand at the end. Your family will. Invest accordingly.

Ask yourself what your children would say about your presence. — Not what you hope they'd say. What they'd actually say. "Dad was always busy." "Dad was always on his phone." "Dad was always tired." Or: "Dad was always there." The honest answer to that question will tell you everything you need to change — or everything you need to keep doing.

List 6: Ten Things to Teach Your Children Before They Leave Your House

How to tell the truth even when it costs them. — The world will offer your children a thousand reasons to lie — to protect themselves, to impress others, to avoid discomfort. Teach them young that the truth is not optional. It is the floor. A lie might get them out of trouble today, but it will build a prison they'll live in for years. Truth-telling is a muscle. Start exercising it early.

How to manage money. — Before they leave your house, your children should know how to budget, save, give, and delay gratification. They should know the difference between a want and a need. They should know that debt is a chain and that contentment is a weapon against everything the world tries to sell them. If they leave your house financially illiterate, the world will educate them — with interest.

How to work without complaining. — Mow the lawn. Wash the car. Clean the kitchen. Not for an allowance — for the principle. Teach them that work is not punishment. It is contribution. It is participation in the life of a household and eventually in the life of a community. A child who learns to work without complaining becomes an adult the world can count on.

How to treat people who can do nothing for them. — The waiter. The janitor. The new kid. The elderly woman in the checkout line. Teach your children that kindness is not strategic — it is standard. That every person they meet carries a weight they cannot see. That the measure of a person's character is not how they treat the powerful, but how they treat the invisible.

How to sit in discomfort without running from it. — Boredom. Awkwardness. Grief. Loneliness. The temptation will always be to numb it — with a screen, a substance, a distraction. Teach your children that discomfort is not an emergency. That sitting in it builds something no shortcut can produce. The child who learns to endure small discomforts becomes the adult who endures the large ones.

How to be alone without being afraid. — A child who cannot be alone with their own thoughts is a child who will always be dependent on noise, people, and devices to feel okay. Teach them to read. To think. To sit in a room without a screen and not panic. Solitude is a skill, and the children who develop it early become adults who are anchored rather than anxious.

How to say they're sorry — and mean it. — Not the forced mumble. Not the "sorry if you were offended." A real apology: "I was wrong. What I did hurt you. I won't do it again." Teach them that apologizing is not losing — it is leading. And that the people who refuse to apologize are the people no one wants to follow.

How to disagree without being cruel. — They will encounter people with different beliefs, different values, different convictions. Teach them that disagreement is not war. That they can hold their ground without tearing another person down. That the goal is not to win the argument but to keep their character intact after it's over.

How to pray. — Not the rote kind. The real kind. The kind where you talk to God like He's actually listening — because He is. Teach them that prayer is not a performance. It is a conversation. It is the one thing they will have access to in every room, every crisis, every season of their lives. Give them this before you give them anything else.

That they are deeply loved — no matter what. — Before they walk out your door for the last time, make sure they know this: your love is not based on their grades, their career, their choices, or their failures. It is unconditional. It is permanent. And it will be waiting for them no matter how far they go or how long they stay away. That knowledge is the most important thing a father can leave in his child's heart.

List 7: Ten Ways to Repair the Damage When You've Failed as a Father

Start by admitting you failed. — Not to a counselor. Not to a friend. To them. To the child you hurt, the teenager you ignored, the adult who still carries the weight of your absence. Look them in the eye — or pick up the phone — and say the words: "I failed you. And I'm sorry." No qualifiers. No excuses. The repair cannot begin until the truth is spoken.

Stop defending the past. — "I was doing the best I could" may be true, but it doesn't heal anything. Your child doesn't need an explanation for why you weren't there. They need to know that you see the gap. That you feel the weight of it. Defending the past protects your ego. Owning the past opens the door.

Don't expect immediate forgiveness. — You may apologize and hear nothing. Or hear anger. Or hear silence that lasts months. That's their right. Forgiveness is not owed to you because you finally showed up. It is a gift — and gifts come on the giver's timeline, not the receiver's. Keep showing up anyway. Consistency after failure is the only evidence that the change is real.

Show up now, even if you didn't show up then. — You missed the games. You missed the recitals. You missed the years. You can't get them back. But you can show up today. To the phone call. To the visit. To the grandchild's birthday. Every act of presence now is a deposit against the debt of the past. It won't erase it. But it will prove that you've changed.

Ask them what they needed and listen to the answer. — "What did you need from me that I didn't give you?" That question takes courage to ask — and more courage to hear. But the answer will tell you exactly where the wound is. And a wound you can see is a wound you can address. Don't guess what they needed. Ask. Then sit in the answer without defending yourself.

Do not put the burden of repair on them. — "Why don't you ever call me?" is not repair. It is blame disguised as longing. The father who failed is the father who reaches out. Who calls first. Who drives across town. Who sends the letter. The child did not create the distance. You did. And the road back is yours to walk.

Be patient with the process. — Rebuilding trust with a child you've wounded is not a single conversation. It is a campaign. Months of consistency. Years of showing up. A lifetime of proving that the man who hurt them is not the man who stands before them now. It's slow. It's humbling. And it's worth every step.

Forgive yourself — but don't do it too quickly. — Sit in the weight of what you missed long enough to let it change you. Cheap self-forgiveness produces no growth. But carrying the guilt forever produces no healing. The balance is this: own what you did, grieve what it cost, and then release it to God — not because you deserve release, but because staying imprisoned helps no one.

Let them set the pace. — Some children will want to reconcile quickly. Others will need years. Some may never come around. That is the consequence of the failure, and a real man accepts consequences without demanding a different outcome. Love them from wherever they'll let you. Close or far. Loud or silent. Love doesn't require proximity to be real.

Become the man now that you should have been then. — The greatest apology is a changed life. Not just words — evidence. Be present. Be sober. Be faithful. Be kind. Be the father now that they needed twenty years ago. You cannot undo the past. But you can live the rest of your life as proof that the past does not have to be the final word.

List 8: Ten Ways to Be the Father You Never Had

Grieve what you didn't get. — Before you can build something new, you have to mourn what was missing. The conversations that never happened. The hand that was never on your shoulder. The voice that never said, "I'm proud of you." That grief is not weakness. It is the foundation of every choice you'll make as a father — because the man who never grieves the absence is destined to repeat it.

Stop waiting to feel ready. — No man feels ready to be a father. Especially the man who had no example. You will not feel qualified. You will not feel prepared. You will not feel enough. Do it anyway. Fatherhood is not a credential you earn — it is a commitment you make. And the willingness to try is already more than what you were given.

Study the fathers you wish you'd had. — Watch the man at church who carries his daughter on his shoulders. Watch the man at the game who cheers without coaching from the sideline. Watch the grandfather who gets on the floor with his grandchildren. These men are your textbook. Learn from them. Ask them questions. Let them mentor you — even if they don't know they are.

Build the traditions your family never had. — Saturday morning pancakes. Christmas Eve by the fire. A walk after dinner. An annual camping trip. These things feel small, but they are the architecture of a childhood. Your children will carry them like treasures

— not because the activities were extraordinary, but because you were there. Every time.

Say the words you never heard. — "I love you." "I'm proud of you." "You did great." "I'm here." "I believe in you." Say them until they feel natural. Say them until your children are so accustomed to hearing them that they assume all fathers talk this way. The words your father never said do not have to die with him. You can resurrect them.

Be physically affectionate. — If no one held you, hold your children. If no one hugged you, hug your children. If no one kissed your forehead at night, kiss theirs. Your body will feel awkward doing it because no one taught you how. Do it anyway. Affection is a language, and you can learn it even if no one ever spoke it to you.

Ask for help. — You don't know what you're doing. That's fine. No one does at first. Find a mentor, a counselor, a pastor, a friend who's further down the road and say, "I need help being a good father." That's not failure. That's the bravest sentence a fatherless man can speak. And the man who hears it will respect you more, not less.

Don't overcorrect by being permissive. — Some fatherless men are so afraid of becoming their own father that they swing to the opposite extreme — no discipline, no boundaries, no structure. That's not love. That's fear. Your children need limits just as much as they need affection. The goal is not to be the opposite of your father. The goal is to be the father your children actually need.

Write the story forward. — Your father's failure is a chapter, not the book. You are writing a new story — one where a man who had nothing becomes a man who gives everything. One where the chain of neglect is broken by a man who chose to stay, to try, to love imperfectly but relentlessly. That story is worth telling. And your children will tell it to their children.

Let God father you. — There is a Father who never left. Who never missed a moment. Who sees every tear, hears every prayer, and has never once looked away. If your earthly father abandoned you, your heavenly Father did not. Let Him fill the places that are still empty. Let Him teach you what fatherhood looks like — because He invented it. And what He builds, no one can break.

List 9: Ten Ways to Lead Your Family Through Crisis

Be honest about what's happening. — Don't sugarcoat it. Don't pretend everything is fine when it's not. Your family can handle truth far better than they can handle the anxiety of sensing that something is wrong while you insist that everything is okay. Be age-appropriate. Be measured. But be honest. A father who tells the truth in crisis becomes the voice his family trusts.

Control your reaction before you control the situation. — Your family is watching your face. Your tone. Your body language. If you spiral, they spiral. If you panic, they panic. You don't have to have the answer in the first five minutes. You have to be steady. Take a breath. Speak calmly. The first thing you stabilize in a crisis is yourself.

Pray out loud with your family. — Not because you feel spiritual. Because you're desperate. And because your children need to see that their father has somewhere to go when his own strength runs out. A father who prays out loud in the storm teaches his children the most important lesson they'll ever learn: that there is someone bigger than the crisis, and that man is not afraid to call on Him.

Make a plan and communicate it clearly. — In crisis, people need two things: information and direction. Tell your family what you know, what you don't know, and what you're going to do next. Even if the plan is incomplete, the act of naming it gives your family something to hold onto. Chaos thrives in silence. Leadership fills the void.

Don't make permanent decisions in temporary pain. — Crisis makes everything feel urgent. It compresses your thinking and narrows your options. Before you quit the job, sell the house, or make the phone call you can't take back — pause. Sleep on it. Talk to someone you trust. The worst decisions of your life will be the ones you made in the first seventy-two hours of a storm.

Protect the daily rhythms. — When the world is falling apart, keep the small things steady. Eat dinner together. Maintain bedtime. Go for the walk. These routines are not trivial during a crisis — they are anchors. Your children draw stability from predictability. And the father who preserves the rhythm tells his family, without words, that the foundation is still solid.

Let your wife carry some of the weight. — You are not the sole load-bearer. She is your partner, not your passenger. Let her into the strategy. Let her speak into the decision. Let her carry what she's able to carry. A man who tries to shield his wife from every ounce of pain doesn't protect her — he isolates her. And isolation in a crisis breeds resentment, not gratitude.

Check on your children individually. — Each child experiences crisis differently. The oldest may go quiet. The youngest may act out. The middle one may pretend nothing is wrong. Don't assume they're fine because they're not crying. Pull each one aside. Ask the question. "How are you doing with all of this?" Then listen. Really listen.

Accept help. — A meal from a neighbor. A phone call from a friend. A visit from a pastor. Crisis is not the time for self-sufficiency. The man who accepts help when he needs it models humility for his family. The man who refuses it models pride. And pride has never carried a family through anything.

Remind them — and yourself — that this will pass. — Not as a dismissal. Not as a platitude. As a truth. Seasons end. Storms break. Morning comes. The crisis feels permanent because you're standing in the middle of it. But your family needs to hear your voice say, "We will get through this. Together." And then they need to watch you live like you believe it.

List 10: Ten Ways to Let Your Children See the Real You

Talk about your own childhood honestly. — Not as a lecture. Not as a cautionary tale. As a window. Tell them about your fears, your friendships, the things you got wrong, the things that shaped you. A child who knows their father's story understands that the man in front of them was once a boy just like them — and that growing up is not something to fear but something to walk through.

Let them see you struggle with something. — Fix the sink and fail. Try the recipe and burn it. Attempt the project and start over. Your children need to see that their father doesn't have it all figured out — and that not having it figured out is not a reason to quit. The struggle is the lesson. And a father who struggles in front of his children gives them permission to do the same.

Tell them what you're afraid of. — Not to burden them. To humanize yourself. "I'm nervous about this meeting." "I'm worried about Grandpa." "I'm scared I'm not getting this right." A father who admits fear doesn't lose authority. He gains trust. Because the child knows: if Dad can be afraid and still show up, then so can I.

Share your faith — including your doubts. — Don't present God to your children as a system you've mastered. Present Him as a relationship you're still learning. Tell them what you believe and why. Tell them the questions you don't have answers to. A father who shares his faith honestly raises children who own their faith, rather than children who borrow one they never examined.

Apologize in front of them. — Not just to them — to their mother, to a friend, to anyone you've wronged. Let them watch you say the words. Let them see that their father is a man who values integrity over image. A public apology from a father teaches a child more about manhood than a thousand private lectures.

Cry when it hurts. — Not for performance. Not to manipulate. Because something genuinely moved you — a funeral, a song, a memory, a moment with your child that overwhelmed you. Tears from a strong man are not a sign of collapse. They are a sign that the man is fully alive. And a child who sees their father cry learns that emotions are not the enemy.

Celebrate your weaknesses. — "I'm terrible at this." "Your mother is way better at that than I am." "I need help with this." A father who can laugh at his own limitations teaches his children that imperfection is not shameful — it is human. The father who pretends to be perfect raises children who are terrified of being anything less.

Let them in on your decisions. — Not every decision. But some. "I've been thinking about whether we should do this. Here's what I'm considering." When you invite your children into your thought process, you're teaching them how to think — not just what to think. Decision-making is a skill, and it's best learned by watching someone do it out loud.

Put down the performance. — Your children don't need a hero. They need a father. A real one. One who burns the toast and forgets the carpool and sometimes loses his patience and then comes back and says, "I'm sorry. I'll do better." The perfect father doesn't exist. The honest one does. And the honest one is the one they'll remember with love.

Be the same person at home that you are everywhere else. — If you're funny at work and silent at home, your children know which version of you is real. If you're patient with strangers and explosive with your family, they know the truth. Consistency between your public and private life is the single greatest gift you can give your children. It tells them that the man they love is not a character. He's real.

FATHERHOOD: QUOTES

"My father gave me the greatest gift anyone could give another person: he believed in me." —Jim Valvano

"Any man can be a father, but it takes someone special to be a dad." —Anne Geddes

"A truly rich man is one whose children run into his arms when his hands are empty." —Author Unknown

"Train up a child in the way he should go: and when he is old, he will not depart from it." —Proverbs 22:6

"The greatest thing a father can do for his children is to love their mother." —Attributed to Theodore Hesburgh

"Fathers, do not provoke your children to anger, but bring them up in the discipline and instruction of the Lord." —Ephesians 6:4

"I cannot think of any need in childhood as strong as the need for a father's protection." —Sigmund Freud

"When you teach your son, you teach your son's son." —The Talmud

"My father didn't tell me how to live. He lived, and let me watch him do it." —Clarence Budington Kelland

"Every father should remember one day his son will follow his example, not his advice." —Charles Kettering

---

FATHERHOOD: PUTTING IT INTO PRACTICE

This week, put your phone in a drawer from dinner until bedtime. — Every night. No exceptions. Two hours of undivided presence. Watch what happens when your children realize they have your full attention — not the scraps between notifications.

Ask each of your children this question: "What's one thing I could do better as your dad?" — And listen. Don't defend. Don't explain. Don't correct. Just receive. What they tell you will be more valuable than anything you read in a parenting book.

Write a letter to each of your children. — Tell them what you see in them. Tell them what you admire. Tell them what you hope for their future. Put it on paper — real paper — and give it to them. A letter from a father is something a child keeps forever.

Identify one daily rhythm with your children and protect it like your life depends on it. — Breakfast together. Bedtime stories. A walk after dinner.

Whatever it is, make it sacred. Cancel everything else before you cancel that.

If you have been an absent father, call your child today. — Don't wait for the right words. Just call. "I've been thinking about you. I miss you. I'm sorry for what I didn't give you." That phone call is the first step on a road you should have walked a long time ago. Take it today.

Sit with your son or daughter for thirty minutes with no screen, no agenda, no activity. — Just be together. Talk if they want to talk. Be silent if they don't. Let them feel what it's like to have a father who is simply present. That thirty minutes will mean more than you think.

Teach your child one practical skill this month. — How to change a tire. How to cook a meal. How to balance a checkbook. How to shake a hand. How to tie a tie. How to look someone in the eye and apologize. These are the things school won't teach them. They're yours to pass on.

Pray with your children before bed this week. — Out loud. In your own words. Not a script — a conversation with God while your child listens. Let them hear their father talk to the God he trusts. That sound will echo in their hearts for the rest of their lives.

If your father failed you, write him a letter — even if you never send it. — Name what he missed. Name what it cost you. Then write this: "I choose to build something different." That letter is not for him. It is for you. And it is the first brick in the house you're building for your own children.

Tell your children you love them every single day this week — out loud, by name. — Not in a text. With your voice. "I love you, [name]." Look them in the eye when you say it. Say it at breakfast. Say it at bedtime. Say it when they leave the house. Never let a day pass where your child has to wonder.

CATEGORY 4

MARRIAGE & DEVOTION

List 1: Ten Ways to Love Your Wife Like She's the Only Woman in the World

Look at her the way you looked at her the first time. — Something dies when a man stops seeing his wife. Not when he stops looking — when he stops seeing. She is still the woman you chose. She is still the woman who chose you back. The years have changed her body, her face, her laugh — and they've changed yours too. But the woman standing in your kitchen is the same woman who made your hands shake the first time you held hers. See her again.

Put her above every other relationship except God. — Not your mother. Not your children. Not your friends. Not your career. She comes first — after your Creator and before everything else. A marriage that is second to anything other than God is a marriage that is slowly being starved. She needs to know — not assume, not hope — that she is your priority. Tell her. Then prove it.

Listen to her like her words are the most important thing you'll hear today. — Not while scrolling. Not while watching the screen over her shoulder. Not while mentally drafting your response before she finishes her sentence. Stop. Turn toward her. Put everything down. A woman who is truly listened to by her husband feels loved in a way that flowers, gifts, and vacations cannot replicate.

Touch her without wanting something. — Hold her hand in the car. Put your arm around her at church. Touch the small of her back when she's standing at the counter. Not every touch has to lead somewhere. Some of the most powerful touches are the ones that say, "I'm here. I'm close. I'm not going anywhere." A woman who is touched with tenderness and no agenda feels safe in her husband's hands.

Speak about her with honor when she's not in the room. — The way you talk about your wife when she's not there tells the world who you really are. If you mock her, belittle her, or roll your eyes when her name comes up — you are not a man who loves his wife. You are a man who performs love when it's convenient. Speak about her the way you'd want another man to speak about your daughter.

Learn her language. — Not her literal language. Her love language. The way she receives love may not be the way you give it. She may need words when you default to actions. She may need presence when you default to gifts. Study her. Ask her. Pay attention. The man who loves his wife in her language — not his — is the man who actually reaches her heart.

Protect her peace. — She carries more than you know. The mental load of the household, the emotional weight of the children, the quiet anxiety she never mentions because she doesn't want to burden you. You cannot carry all of it for her, but you can lighten it. Take something off her plate. Handle the thing she's been dreading. Shield her from the noise. A man who protects his wife's peace is a man who loves her in the place she needs it most.

Choose her every single day. — Marriage is not a one-time decision. It is a daily one. Every morning you wake up and choose her again — her imperfections, her moods, her history, her complexity. The man who says "I chose you once" is a man who stopped choosing. The man who says "I choose you today" is a man who understands what devotion actually means.

Never stop pursuing her. — The pursuit didn't end at the altar. It began there. Date her. Surprise her. Write her a note she doesn't expect. Ask her questions you haven't asked in years. The moment you stop pursuing your wife is the moment the marriage shifts from alive to autopilot — and autopilot always drifts.

Pray for her. — Not just when things are hard. Every day. Pray for her health, her peace, her joy, her purpose, her faith. Pray for the parts of her life you cannot touch with your hands. A man who prays for his wife has taken the most important part of his marriage — her soul — and placed it in the hands of the only One who can truly protect it.

List 2: Ten Things That Will Destroy Your Marriage If You Let Them

The screen you choose over her face. — It starts small. A scroll during dinner. A show after the kids go to bed. A notification checked mid-sentence. And slowly, imperceptibly, the device in your hand becomes the third person in your marriage — the one who gets your best attention, your final thoughts at night, and your first glance in the morning. She notices. She always notices. And the distance between your screen and her heart grows wider every night you choose the glow over the woman beside you.

The words you say in anger that you can never take back. — You can apologize. You can explain. You can regret it for years. But once you've called her a name, once you've said the cruelest thing you could think of in the heat of the moment — it lives in her memory forever. She may forgive you. She will not forget. A man who cannot control his mouth in conflict is a man who is slowly demolishing the safest place his wife has.

The comparison to other women. — Whether it's the woman on the screen, the woman at the office, or the woman in your imagination — every time you measure your wife against someone else, you have told her she is not enough. Comparison is the acid that dissolves gratitude. And a marriage without gratitude is a marriage waiting to collapse.

The silence that replaces communication. — Not every silence is peaceful. Some silence is punishment. Some silence is avoidance. Some silence is the slow withdrawal of a man who has decided it's easier to say nothing than to do the work of honest conversation. When you stop talking to your wife — really talking — you have stopped building the marriage. And anything you stop building starts to decay.

The resentment you carry instead of addressing. — She did something three years ago that hurt you, and you never said a word. You buried it. And now it leaks out sideways — in sarcasm, in coldness, in the way you sigh when she asks you a question. Resentment is not patience. It is poison with a long fuse. Say what needs to be said. Say it kindly. But say it. The marriage cannot heal what you refuse to name.

The friendships you won't set boundaries around. — Not every friendship is a threat. But some are. The coworker who texts too late. The ex who still calls. The friend who doesn't respect your wife. A man who refuses to draw boundaries around the relationships outside his marriage is a man who has left the front door unlocked and wonders why the house feels unsafe.

The refusal to grow. — She's reading. She's reflecting. She's trying to be a better wife, a better mother, a better person. And you're standing still. A marriage where one person is growing and the other refuses to will eventually snap from the tension. Growth is not optional. It is the oxygen of a living relationship. The day you stop growing is the day the marriage starts dying.

The pornography you think she doesn't know about. — She knows. Or she suspects. And even if she doesn't — it is rewiring your brain, eroding your intimacy, and teaching you to see women as objects instead of people. There is no version of this that doesn't damage your marriage. None. A man who feeds his eyes in secret starves his wife in the open. And the hunger she feels is not one she can name — but it is one she carries every day.

The financial secrets. — The account she doesn't know about. The debt you haven't mentioned. The purchase you hid. Financial dishonesty is not a money problem — it is a trust problem. And trust, once fractured by secrecy, takes years to rebuild. Be transparent. Share the numbers. Share the stress. A marriage built on hidden ledgers is a marriage built on sand.

The assumption that the marriage will survive on autopilot. — It won't. A marriage that is not being actively nurtured is a marriage that is slowly dying. You cannot coast on the love you felt ten years ago. Love is a living thing — it requires feeding, attention, effort, and sacrifice. The man who assumes his marriage is fine because nothing is visibly broken is the man who will be blindsided when the cracks finally show.

List 3: Ten Ways to Fight Fair and Never Fight Dirty

Agree that the goal is resolution, not victory. — The moment you start trying to win the argument, you've already lost the marriage. You are not opponents. You are partners who disagree. The question is not "How do I prove I'm right?" The question is "How do we get to the other side of this together?" If she loses, you lose. Every time.

Never raise your voice. — Volume is not conviction. It is intimidation. And a woman who is shouted at by the man she loves does not hear the argument. She hears the threat. Lower your voice. Speak slowly. Say less. The quieter you become in conflict, the more clearly she can hear you — and the safer she feels disagreeing with you.

Stay in the room. — Walking out mid-argument is not self-control. It is abandonment in the moment she needs you most. If you need to pause, say so. "I need ten minutes to cool down. I'm not leaving — I just need a moment." That's different from slamming the door and driving away. Stay. Even when staying is harder than running.

Fight about the issue, not the person. — "You forgot to pay the bill" is an issue. "You always forget everything — you're so irresponsible" is an attack. The moment you move from the behavior to the character, the conversation is no longer about the bill. It's about her worth. And no woman should have her worth questioned by the man who vowed to protect it.

Ban the word 'always' and the word 'never.' — "You always do this." "You never listen." These words are grenades, and they blow up every good thing she's ever done. They erase her effort and replace it with a permanent accusation. Be specific. Be honest. But do not use language that rewrites her entire history in the shadow of one disagreement.

Don't bring her family into it. — "You're just like your mother." That sentence has destroyed more marriages than infidelity. Her family is her blood. Even if she complains about them, you don't get to. And using her family as a weapon in an argument tells her that you see her not as an individual but as an extension of people she didn't choose to be born to. Leave them out of it. Always.

Never threaten the marriage. — "Maybe we should just get a divorce." "Maybe you'd be happier with someone else." These words, even spoken in frustration, plant seeds of insecurity that grow roots in the dark. If you don't mean it, don't say it. And if you do mean it, say it to a counselor, not in the middle of a fight about dishes. The word "divorce" should never be used as a weapon. It should never be casual. It should never be thrown.

Apologize before the sun goes down. — You will not always resolve the conflict in one conversation. But you can always take ownership of your part before the day ends. "I'm sorry for how I spoke to you. I was wrong. I don't want to go to bed with this between us." That sentence costs your pride everything. And it gives your marriage exactly what it needs.

Touch her during the fight. — Not aggressively. Not to shut her down. But a hand on her knee, a gentle touch on her arm — something that says, "I'm frustrated, but I'm not going anywhere." Physical connection during conflict disarms the fear that lives beneath every argument: the fear that this fight might be the one that ends everything. Your touch says it won't.

Debrief after the storm passes. — Once the emotions settle, come back to it. "What did we learn? What do we need to change? How can we fight better next time?" A marriage that never processes its conflicts is a marriage that keeps fighting the same war. The debrief is where the real growth happens — when the heat is gone and the honesty can breathe.

List 4: Ten Ways to Protect Your Marriage from the Outside

Guard your eyes. — What you look at shapes what you want. And what you want shapes what you pursue. A man who feeds his eyes on images of other women — on a screen, on a billboard, in his imagination — is slowly training his desire to look anywhere but home. Guard what enters your eyes the way you'd guard the front door of your house. Because what comes in through the eyes eventually walks into the marriage.

Guard your conversations. — The woman at work who laughs at your jokes. The old friend who understands you. The stranger online who makes you feel seen. Emotional affairs don't begin with physical contact. They begin with conversations you wouldn't have if your wife were sitting beside you. If you're saying things to another woman that you wouldn't say in front of your wife, you've already crossed a line.

Stop complaining about your wife to other people.
— When you vent about your marriage to a friend, a
coworker, or a stranger on the internet, you are not
relieving pressure. You are recruiting allies against the
woman you promised to protect. Your frustration
belongs in two places: between you and your wife, or
between you and a counselor. Nowhere else.

Set boundaries with technology. — Shared
passwords. No secret accounts. No private messages
that your spouse couldn't read. These are not signs of
distrust — they are acts of transparency. A man who
needs digital privacy from his wife is a man who is
hiding something. Openness is not a sacrifice. It is a
safeguard.

**Limit the friendships that don't respect your
marriage.** — If a friend encourages you to look at
other women, mocks your commitment, or invites you
into situations your wife wouldn't approve of — that
friend is not sharpening you. He is eroding you. A man
who protects his marriage protects it from every
direction — including from the men who don't value
theirs.

Don't let your parents undermine your wife. —
When you got married, you left your father and mother.
That's not a suggestion — it's a command. If your
mother criticizes your wife and you stay silent, you
have chosen the wrong side. Your wife needs to know
that you will stand between her and anyone who
threatens her place in your life — including the woman
who raised you.

Make your marriage visible. — Hold her hand in public. Speak well of her at dinner parties. Post about her on your anniversary — not for the audience, but for her. When the world sees a man who is proud of his wife, it creates a barrier that affairs, temptation, and outside interference have a harder time penetrating. Visibility is protection.

Never entertain the fantasy of someone else. — The moment you allow your mind to imagine life with another woman — even briefly, even "harmlessly" — you have opened a door that is very hard to close. Fantasy is not innocent. It is rehearsal. And what you rehearse in your mind, you eventually pursue with your hands. Shut it down the moment it enters. Every time.

Keep the marriage off social media during conflict. — Do not post passive-aggressive quotes. Do not change your status. Do not broadcast your pain to an audience that has no business in your bedroom. Your marriage is not content. It is not entertainment. It is a covenant — and covenants are not subject to public commentary.

Invest in your marriage before it needs saving. — Don't wait for the crisis to book the counselor, schedule the date night, or have the conversation. The marriages that survive are the ones that were being maintained long before the cracks appeared. Change the oil before the engine seizes. The same principle applies to the most important relationship of your life.

List 5: Ten Ways to Lead Your Home Without Controlling It

Lead by serving, not by commanding. — The greatest leader who ever lived got on His knees and washed the feet of His followers. That is your model. Not the man who barks orders from the recliner. Not the man who demands dinner on the table and silence in the house. The man who leads his home is the man who rolls up his sleeves and does the work no one asked him to do. Authority is not inherited by position. It is earned by sacrifice.

Make decisions with your wife, not for her. — She is your partner, not your subordinate. The man who makes every decision unilaterally and then informs his wife is not leading — he is ruling. There is a difference. Leadership says, "What do you think?" Ruling says, "Here's what I've decided." One builds trust. The other builds resentment.

Create an environment where she can speak freely. — If your wife is afraid to disagree with you, you have not led your home — you have silenced it. A well-led home is one where every voice is heard, where disagreement is safe, and where the strongest person in the room is the one who listens most. Your authority is not threatened by her opinion. It is strengthened by it.

Set the emotional temperature. — If you walk in the door angry, the house becomes angry. If you walk in the door anxious, the house becomes anxious. A man who leads his home understands that his mood is contagious — and he takes responsibility for what he spreads. You are the thermostat, not the thermometer. Set the temperature you want your family to live in.

Carry the weight without making everyone watch you carry it. — Leadership includes burden-bearing. Financial stress. Work pressure. Personal struggles. Carry them — that's your role. But don't carry them loudly. Don't sigh every time you pay a bill. Don't narrate your exhaustion every evening. Your family needs to know you're strong enough to carry the weight without being crushed by it. That doesn't mean you hide — it means you carry with dignity.

Let your wife lead where she's stronger. — A man who must be in charge of everything is not a leader — he is an insecure man with a title. If she is better with finances, let her manage them. If she is better with schedules, let her run them. Leadership is not about being the best at everything. It is about building a team that functions at its highest level — and that means getting out of the way when someone else is more equipped.

Discipline the children together. — Do not be the absent enforcer who only shows up when punishment is needed. Be involved in the daily shaping, the conversations, the corrections. And when discipline is required, present a united front. A home where Mom is the daily parent and Dad is the occasional judge is not a well-led home. It is a divided one.

Be the first to sacrifice. — The last portion of food. The uncomfortable seat. The earlier alarm. The harder conversation. The man who leads his home is the man who takes the smaller piece and gives the larger one to his family. Sacrifice is not martyrdom — it is the daily, invisible proof that you value them more than yourself.

Keep your promises. — Every broken promise — to your wife, to your children — erodes the foundation of your authority. If you say you'll be there, be there. If you say you'll fix it, fix it. If you say things will change, change them. A man's word is the brick his family builds their trust on. And a house built on broken bricks will not stand.

Point the family toward something bigger than yourself. — The best-led homes are not centered on the father. They are centered on God, on purpose, on service, on a vision that outlasts any one person. Lead your family toward faith, toward generosity, toward character. The man who makes himself the center of the home builds a kingdom. The man who makes God the center builds a legacy.

List 6: Ten Ways to Be Emotionally Available When Everything in You Wants to Shut Down

Recognize the shutdown before it completes. — You know the feeling. The walls going up. The jaw tightening. The retreat into silence. Most men don't even realize they're shutting down until the door is already closed. Learn your signals — the physical cues, the emotional triggers, the moments where you begin to check out. Naming the shutdown is the first step to stopping it.

Tell her what's happening instead of going silent.
— "I'm shutting down right now. I can feel it. I need a
minute, but I'm not leaving." That sentence changes
everything. It replaces the terrifying silence — the kind
she interprets as rejection — with honest information.
She can work with honesty. She cannot work with a
wall.

Stop treating emotions as the enemy. —
Somewhere along the way, you were taught that
feelings are liabilities. That real men don't feel. That
the safest place to be is numb. It's a lie — and it's
killing your marriage. Your emotions are not weakness.
They are information. They are telling you something
your logic hasn't caught up to yet. Listen to them.

Answer the question she's actually asking. — When
she says, "Are you okay?" she is not asking for a status
report. She is asking, "Are we okay? Are you still with
me? Do you still love me?" Hear the real question. And
answer it — not with "I'm fine," but with the truth. "I'm
struggling, but I'm here. And I love you." That's what
she needs.

**Stay in the conversation ten minutes longer than
you want to.** — The moment you want to walk away is
usually the moment the conversation is about to break
through. Staying is painful. Staying requires the kind of
endurance that most men reserve for physical
challenges. But the emotional breakthrough — the
moment she feels truly heard and you feel truly known
— happens on the other side of the discomfort you
wanted to avoid.

Let her see the sadness, not just the anger. — Men are trained to convert every emotion into anger because anger feels powerful. Sadness feels exposed. But your wife doesn't need your anger. She needs your honesty. And underneath the anger — almost always — is sadness, fear, or hurt. Let her see that layer. It's the one she can actually meet you in.

Stop fixing and start feeling. — She tells you about her day. She tells you about the argument with her friend. She tells you about the thing that made her cry. And your instinct is to solve it. Resist. She doesn't need a solution. She needs you to say, "That sounds really hard. I'm sorry you went through that." Empathy before engineering. Every time.

Initiate the emotional conversation. — Don't wait for her to ask. Don't wait for the fight to force it. Walk into the room and say, "I want to talk about something. I've been carrying this and I think you should know." That sentence is the opposite of shutdown. It is the sound of a man choosing to open the door instead of bricking it shut.

Understand that emotional availability is not a personality trait — it is a discipline. — You may not be wired for deep conversation. You may not have grown up in a home where feelings were discussed. That's fine. Emotional availability is not about being naturally open. It is about choosing to be open even when every instinct tells you to close. It is a muscle. Build it.

Remember what's at stake. — Every time you shut down, she feels alone. Every time you go silent, she fills the silence with her worst fears. Every time you check out, the distance between you grows — and distance, left unchecked, becomes the permanent architecture of a marriage. What's at stake is not your comfort. It is her heart. And her heart was entrusted to you. Stay open for it.

List 7: Ten Ways to Rebuild Trust After You've Broken It

Tell the whole truth. — Not the version that makes you look less guilty. Not the partial confession that leaves the worst parts buried. The whole truth. All of it. Because she will find out eventually — and when she does, the original betrayal will pale in comparison to the lie you told to cover it. Rip the bandage off. Let her see the wound. Full disclosure is the only foundation strong enough to rebuild on.

Accept the consequences without negotiating. — She's angry. She's cold. She doesn't trust you. She checks your phone. She asks where you've been. Accept it. All of it. You created this. The consequence is not punishment — it is the natural result of broken trust. A man who demands to be trusted before he's earned it back is a man who doesn't understand what he destroyed.

Stop saying "I've changed" and start proving it. — Words are free. Behavior is expensive. The woman you hurt does not need another speech. She needs months of consistent, observable, undeniable evidence that the man who broke her trust is not the man standing in front of her now. Change is not declared. It is demonstrated. Over time. Without exception.

Answer every question she asks — no matter how many times she asks it. — She will ask the same question four different ways on four different nights. She is not trying to punish you. She is trying to understand. She is trying to rebuild the story in her mind so that the world makes sense again. Answer patiently. Answer completely. Answer as if it's the first time she's asked — because in her mind, she's still searching for the piece that makes it click.

Give her access to everything. — Phone. Email. Accounts. Calendar. Location. Not because she demands it. Because you offer it. Transparency is not a prison. It is the scaffolding that holds the structure up while the foundation is being repoured. A man who resists transparency after betrayal is a man who is protecting the very thing that caused the damage.

Do not rush her healing. — You want this to be over. You want the marriage to feel normal again. You want her to stop bringing it up. That's your need — not hers. Her healing will take as long as it takes, and the moment you try to accelerate it is the moment she feels dismissed all over again. Be patient. This is the long road. Walk it without complaining.

Get outside help. — You cannot rebuild a marriage you shattered with the same tools you used to break it. Find a counselor. Join a group. Talk to a pastor. A man who is too proud to ask for help is a man who is too proud to save his marriage. And pride, left unchecked, will cost you more than the betrayal ever did.

Stop blaming the circumstances. — "I was stressed." "She wasn't meeting my needs." "It just happened." None of these are reasons. They are excuses. And excuses tell your wife that you still don't fully own what you did. Own it. Without conditions. Without deflection. Without blaming the context that surrounded the choice. The choice was yours. Say so.

Rebuild the small things first. — You cannot go from betrayal to intimacy in one step. Start with the small things. Make her coffee. Be home when you say you'll be home. Follow through on the mundane promises. Trust is rebuilt in the ordinary, not the extraordinary. It's the Tuesday-night consistency that convinces her — not the anniversary grand gesture.

Understand that you may carry this scar for life. — She may forgive you. The marriage may survive. But the memory will remain — a tender spot that flares up on bad days, a shadow that crosses her face when something reminds her. Accept it. Carry it with humility. And let it serve as the permanent reminder that trust is the most valuable thing you have — and the most expensive thing to replace.

List 8: Ten Ways to Keep the Fire Alive After the Honeymoon Ends

Date her like you're still trying to win her. — You won her once. Now win her again. And again. And again. Not because she's keeping score, but because a woman who feels pursued by her husband feels alive in her marriage. Plan the dinner. Open the door. Dress like you care. Look at her like the room just got brighter when she walked in. She deserves that — not just once, but for life.

Talk about something other than the kids and the bills. — Somewhere between the wedding and the present, the conversations shrank. They became logistical. Schedules. Errands. Problems to solve. Those conversations are necessary, but they are not nourishing. Ask her about her dreams. Tell her about yours. Talk about the book she's reading, the memory that made you laugh, the thing you want to build together. Feed the marriage with conversation that has nothing to do with management.

Touch her every day. — Not just in the bedroom. In the hallway. At the counter. In the car. A kiss that lasts two seconds longer than usual. A hand on her waist when you pass her. A hug that isn't rushed. Daily physical connection is the pulse of a marriage — and when the touching stops, the distance starts.

Laugh together. — The couples who last are the couples who still make each other laugh. Watch something funny together. Remind each other of the ridiculous thing that happened on your honeymoon. Be silly. Be playful. Laughter is not trivial — it is oxygen. And a marriage that stops laughing is a marriage that has started holding its breath.

Protect your time alone together. — The children will consume every hour you let them. So will work, church, friends, and obligations. You must carve out time for just the two of you — and you must defend it like it matters. Because it does. A weekly date, a monthly overnight, an annual trip — whatever the rhythm, make it sacred. Your marriage is not the leftovers. It is the main course.

Surprise her. — Not with expensive things. With thoughtful ones. A note in her bag. Her favorite coffee waiting on the counter. A text in the middle of the day that says, "I was thinking about you." Surprise is the antidote to routine. It tells your wife that she's still on your mind even when she's not in the room. That alone is enough to keep a fire burning.

Be curious about who she's becoming. — She is not the same woman you married. She has grown, changed, deepened. Are you paying attention? Ask her what she's been thinking about. Ask her what she wants to learn. Ask her what she's afraid of now that she wasn't afraid of then. A marriage that stays curious stays connected. The one that assumes it already knows everything is the one that goes cold.

Flirt with her. — Yes, after twenty years. Yes, with kids in the house. Yes, even when you're tired. Flirting is not a phase of the relationship — it is the heartbeat. The wink across the room. The whisper in her ear. The playful comment that makes her blush. A woman who is flirted with by her husband feels desired — and desire is one of the most powerful forces in a marriage.

Pray together. — This is the most intimate thing two people can do — and the one most couples avoid. Get on your knees together. Hold her hand. Pray out loud. Not long prayers. Not perfect ones. Just honest ones. A couple that prays together builds a bond that no argument, no crisis, and no season of distance can sever. Do it tonight.

Remember why you chose her. — On the hard days — the days when the marriage feels more like work than wonder — go back to the beginning. Why her? What was it about her that made you certain she was the one? That reason hasn't changed. It's still there, buried under the years and the routines and the weight of daily life. Dig it up. Hold it in your hands. And let it remind you that what you have is worth every ounce of effort it takes to keep it alive.

List 9: Ten Ways to Honor Your Wife in Public and in Private

Speak well of her in front of your children. — Your children are forming their understanding of marriage by watching yours. If they hear you praise their mother, they learn that a man honors his wife. If they hear you criticize her, mock her, or dismiss her — they learn that, too. What you say about your wife in front of your children is not a comment. It is curriculum.

Open the door. — The car door. The restaurant door. The door to the house. It is not outdated. It is not performative. It is a small, physical declaration that says, "You go first. I'll hold this for you." A woman who is treated with courtesy by her husband in public feels valued. And a man who extends it without being asked proves that honor is not an event — it is a habit.

Defend her when someone disrespects her. — If someone speaks poorly of your wife — a family member, a coworker, a stranger — you shut it down. Immediately. You don't laugh along. You don't stay silent. You make it clear, in whatever tone the moment requires, that the woman they are talking about is under your protection. Silence in the face of disrespect is agreement with it.

Brag about her in rooms she'll never enter. — At the office. At the gym. At dinner with friends. Tell people how incredible she is. Not to perform — to declare. The man who speaks about his wife with pride in rooms she will never enter is a man who truly sees her. And even though she'll never hear those specific words, the way you carry yourself after saying them will tell her everything.

Never correct her in front of other people. — If she gets a fact wrong at dinner, let it go. If she tells a story differently than you remember it, let it go. The moment you correct your wife publicly, you have prioritized being right over being kind — and the people at the table will remember your correction long after they've forgotten the fact. Save it for the car ride home. Or better yet, let it go entirely.

Serve her in the quiet moments. — Refill her water glass without being asked. Fold the laundry she forgot about. Handle the errand she was dreading. These are not grand romantic gestures. They are small, invisible acts of devotion — and they are the truest measure of honor. The man who serves when no one is watching is the man who honors his wife at the deepest level.

Make her feel beautiful. — Not once a year on her birthday. Regularly. Specifically. "You look incredible in that dress." "Your eyes are the first thing I notice every morning." "You're the most beautiful woman I've ever seen." She hears a thousand messages every day telling her she's not enough. Let your voice be the loudest one in her life — and let it say the opposite.

Give her space to be imperfect. — She will burn dinner. She will forget the appointment. She will lose her patience with the kids. She will have a bad day and take it out on the wrong person. And in those moments, the man who honors his wife is the man who says, "It's okay. I'm not going anywhere." Grace in the imperfect moments is the truest form of honor — because it mirrors the grace you've been given yourself.

Be faithful — in every room, on every screen, with every thought. — Faithfulness is not just the absence of an affair. It is the presence of devotion in every corner of your life. In what you watch. In what you think. In how you interact with every woman who is not your wife. The man who is faithful only in public is not faithful at all. The man who is faithful in the dark is the man his wife can trust completely.

Tell her you love her like you mean it. — Not as a reflex. Not as a goodbye at the door. Look her in the eye. Hold her face. Say the words slowly, like they cost you something. "I love you." Those three words, spoken with intention, are not a habit. They are a vow renewed. And a woman who hears them — really hears them — from the man she married will carry them like armor into every hard thing she faces.

List 10: Ten Ways to Be the Husband She Deserves Even When You Don't Feel Like It

Show up anyway. — There will be nights when you are exhausted. Mornings when you have nothing left. Seasons when the romance feels like a distant memory and the marriage feels like a job. Show up anyway. Not because you feel like it. Because you committed to it. Feelings follow action. They rarely lead it. And the man who waits until he feels like being a good husband will wait his whole life.

Do the thing she's been asking for. — She's asked you three times to fix the faucet. She's mentioned the date night she wants. She's told you she needs you to come home earlier. You heard her. You just haven't moved. Move. Today. Not because the task is urgent, but because her voice deserves a response — and every ignored request teaches her that her words don't carry weight in your house.

Choose kindness over being right. — You're right. You're technically, factually, objectively right. And she's still hurt. In that moment, being right doesn't matter. Being kind does. The marriage doesn't need a winner. It needs a man who can set his ego down long enough to say, "I hear you. I'm sorry this is hard." Kindness after disagreement is one of the most difficult and most important things a husband can offer.

Go to bed at the same time. — It sounds simple. It's not. One of you scrolls while the other sleeps. One of you works late while the other lies awake. The bed is the last shared space of the day — and the couples who protect it are the couples who stay connected. Put the device away. Get under the covers at the same time. That shared quiet, night after night, builds something no separate schedule ever will.

Initiate the conversation you've been avoiding. — There's something sitting between you. You both feel it. Neither of you wants to name it. Be the man who names it. "I know we haven't been right. I want to talk about it." That sentence takes courage. It also takes the marriage off life support and gives it a chance to breathe. The conversation you're avoiding is the conversation the marriage needs most.

Be generous with your time. — Time is the one thing you cannot refund. Give it to her. Sit on the porch. Take the walk. Listen to the story she's told twice before like you're hearing it for the first time. The man who is generous with his time is the man who is generous with his love — because time is the currency love is measured in.

Stop keeping score. — "I did the dishes last night." "I'm the one who always picks up the kids." "I took out the trash — what did you do?" The moment your marriage becomes a ledger, it has stopped being a partnership. Give without counting. Serve without tracking. Love without calculating who owes what. The scoreboard has no place in a covenant.

Compliment her when she least expects it. — On a Tuesday morning. In the middle of the grocery run. While she's washing her face at night. Not on Valentine's Day when it's expected, but on the random Wednesday when it's not. "I love the life we've built together." "You're a better mom than you think you are." "I'd marry you again tomorrow." Unexpected words land the hardest — and they stay the longest.

Protect her rest. — Take the baby at 5 a.m. Let her sleep in on Saturday. Handle the kids for an hour so she can be alone with her own thoughts. A wife who is rested is a wife who has the energy to love, to connect, to be present. A wife who is perpetually exhausted is a wife who is slowly running on empty — and a husband who doesn't notice is a husband who isn't paying attention.

Renew the vow in your heart every morning. — Not the ceremony. The commitment. Before your feet hit the floor, decide: today I will love her well. Today I will be patient. Today I will listen. Today I will serve. Today I will be the husband she deserves — not because she earned it this morning, but because I made a promise. And my promises don't expire with my mood.

MARRIAGE & DEVOTION: QUOTES

"Husbands, love your wives, just as Christ loved the church and gave himself up for her." —Ephesians 5:25

"A successful marriage requires falling in love many times, always with the same person." —Mignon McLaughlin

"The greatest thing you'll ever learn is just to love and be loved in return." —Eden Ahbez

"Let all that you do be done in love." —1 Corinthians 16:14

"He who finds a wife finds a good thing and obtains favor from the Lord." —Proverbs 18:22

"In marriage, each partner is to be an encourager rather than a critic, a forgiver rather than a collector of hurts, an enabler rather than a reformer." —H. Norman Wright

"Love is patient, love is kind. It does not envy, it does not boast, it is not proud. It does not dishonor others, it is not self-seeking, it is not easily angered, it keeps no record of wrongs." —1 Corinthians 13:4-5

"There is no more lovely, friendly, and charming relationship, communion, or company than a good marriage." —Martin Luther

"The real act of marriage takes place in the heart, not in the ballroom or church or synagogue. It's a choice you make — not just on your wedding day, but over and over again — and that choice is reflected in the way you treat your husband or wife." —Barbara De Angelis

"What therefore God has joined together, let not man separate." —Mark 10:9

MARRIAGE & DEVOTION: PUTTING IT INTO PRACTICE

Tonight, put every device in another room from dinner until bed. — Give your wife your full, undivided attention. No exceptions. Watch what happens when the screen isn't competing for the space between you.

Ask your wife this question: "When do you feel most loved by me?" — Then listen. The answer may surprise you. Whatever she says, do more of it this week. Her answer is the blueprint for the marriage she needs.

Write her a handwritten note and leave it where she'll find it. — Not a text. A note. On paper. In your handwriting. Tell her something you haven't said in a while. It takes three minutes. She'll keep it for thirty years.

Schedule a date night this week — and protect it like a work meeting. — No kids. No screens. No logistics. Just the two of you, face to face, remembering why you chose each other. If money is tight, take a walk. If time is short, go for coffee. The activity doesn't matter. The intention does.

Identify one thing she's been asking you to do — and do it today. — Don't announce it. Don't wait for recognition. Just do it. The faucet. The phone call. The conversation. Action without fanfare is one of the purest expressions of love a husband can offer.

Go to bed at the same time every night this week. — Turn off the screen. Lie beside her. Talk or don't talk — but be there. The last five minutes of the day, shared in the same bed at the same time, builds more intimacy than a weekend getaway.

Pray for your wife by name every morning this week. — Before your feet hit the floor. Pray for her peace, her joy, her health, her faith. Pray for the parts of her life you can't touch with your hands. And if you're brave enough — tell her you're doing it.

This week, compliment your wife once a day at a moment she doesn't expect. — Not when she's dressed up. When she's in sweats. When she's driving. When she's folding laundry. When the compliment is least expected, it's most believed.

Ask her: "Is there anything I've done recently that I need to apologize for?" — And mean it. Don't get defensive. Don't explain. Just hear it, own it, and say, "I'm sorry." A man who invites accountability from his wife is a man who values the marriage more than his ego.

Sit across from your wife and tell her: "I'd choose you again." — Hold her hands. Look her in the eye. Say it slowly. Mean every word. That sentence, spoken with weight and sincerity, can repair more damage than a year of counseling. Try it tonight.

CATEGORY 5

LEADERSHIP

List 1: Ten Ways to Lead When Nobody Gave You Permission

Stop waiting to be chosen. — Most men are standing in line, hoping someone will tap them on the shoulder and say, "It's your turn." That tap is not coming. Leadership is not an appointment — it is a decision.

The man who waits for permission to lead will spend his life following men who were simply willing to go first. If you see something that needs to be done, do it. That's how leadership begins — not with a title, but with a step.

Be the first to act. — In every room, every crisis, every awkward silence — someone goes first. Let it be you. Not because you have the best plan. Not because you're the most qualified. Because someone has to move, and the man who moves first sets the direction for everyone else. Action in the absence of certainty is one of the purest forms of leadership.

Take responsibility for things you didn't cause. — The leader doesn't ask, "Whose fault was this?" He asks, "What do we do now?" When you take ownership of a problem that isn't yours, you tell everyone in the room that you care more about the outcome than the blame. That's the moment people start following you — not when you assign fault, but when you absorb it.

Solve problems before anyone asks you to. — The man who identifies a problem, develops a solution, and presents both without being asked has just led — whether anyone noticed or not. Leadership is not about visibility. It is about initiative. The most powerful leaders in any organization are often the ones whose names never appear on the marquee because they were too busy doing the work.

Lead from wherever you are. — You don't need the corner office. You don't need the fancy title. You don't need to be the oldest, the loudest, or the most experienced. You need to be the most willing. The man who leads from the mailroom with integrity will eventually lead from the boardroom with authority. Position follows character. Not the other way around.

Be the one who speaks up when everyone else is silent. — There will be moments — in meetings, in neighborhoods, in families — when something needs to be said and no one is saying it. The easy thing is to stay quiet. The leadership thing is to open your mouth. Not to dominate — to serve. The man who speaks the truth when silence is the safer option is the man the room will remember.

Invest in the people around you. — Leadership without investment is just management. Learn the names of the people you work with. Ask about their families. Notice when they're struggling. Offer your time, your knowledge, your encouragement. A leader who pours into people doesn't need to demand loyalty. He earns it — one genuine conversation at a time.

Do the work no one wants to do. — The man who picks up the trash, who stays late to finish the project, who volunteers for the thankless task — that man is leading. Not from the front of the stage, but from the trenches. And the people who see it — and they always see it — will follow him long before they follow the man who only shows up for the spotlight.

Be consistent. — Anyone can lead on a good day. The man who leads on the bad days — when he's tired, when the results aren't there, when the team is struggling — that's the man people trust. Consistency is the currency of leadership. It is the proof that your character is not dependent on your circumstances.

Give credit away like it costs you nothing. — Because it doesn't. The leader who hoards credit builds resentment. The leader who distributes it builds loyalty. "We did this" will always be more powerful than "I did this." The man who points at his team when things go right — and points at himself when things go wrong — is the man no one wants to stop following.

List 2: Ten Ways to Earn Respect Without Demanding It

Keep your word. — Every time. Without exception. A man who does what he says he will do — when he says he will do it — earns a respect that no title, no position, and no paycheck can buy. People don't respect your intentions. They respect your follow-through. And follow-through, done consistently over years, is the single most powerful reputation builder a man has.

Show up early. — Not to impress anyone. To demonstrate that you value other people's time. The man who arrives early has already told the room, before saying a word, that this matters to him. It is a small act that carries enormous weight — because in a world of late arrivals and casual delays, punctuality has become a form of leadership.

Treat the janitor the same way you treat the CEO. — Respect that adjusts based on rank is not respect. It is strategy. The man who shakes every hand with the same firmness, looks every person in the eye with the same attention, and speaks to every human being with the same dignity — that man earns a reputation that no performance review can manufacture.

Admit what you don't know. — The insecure man pretends to have every answer. The respected man says, "I don't know, but I'll find out." Admitting ignorance is not a weakness — it is a trust accelerator. People don't need you to be omniscient. They need you to be honest. And honesty about your limitations earns more respect than any bluff ever will.

Stay calm when everyone else is rattled. — Panic is contagious. So is composure. The man who keeps his voice steady, his thinking clear, and his emotions controlled when the world is shaking becomes the man everyone looks to. You don't earn respect by reacting the fastest. You earn it by reacting the best. And the best reaction, in almost every crisis, is measured calm.

Do what's right even when it's expensive. — Return the money. Report the error. Refuse the shortcut. Walk away from the deal that doesn't feel clean. Integrity is not a philosophy — it is a practice. And the man who practices it when it costs him something earns a respect that the man who only practices it when it's convenient will never touch.

Listen more than you speak. — The man who listens is the man who learns. And the man who learns is the man who leads with insight instead of assumption. When you sit in a conversation and genuinely listen — not waiting for your turn, not formulating your response — you honor the person across from you. And honored people give respect freely.

Take the blame. — When the project fails, when the plan falls apart, when the mistake costs the team — stand up and own it. Even if it wasn't entirely your fault. Especially if it wasn't entirely your fault. A man who absorbs blame protects his team. And a team that feels protected will follow that man through anything.

Live the same life in public and in private. — The fastest way to lose respect is to be caught being two different people. The man who is charming at the conference and cruel at home. The man who preaches generosity and hoards his money. The man who talks about integrity and cuts corners when no one is looking. Respect is built on consistency — and consistency means the public man and the private man are the same person.

Respect others first. — Respect is not a commodity to be traded. It is a seed to be planted. The man who extends respect before it's been earned — to the new employee, to the stranger, to the person who disagrees with him — creates an environment where respect grows naturally. You don't command respect. You cultivate it. And cultivation always starts with what you put in the ground, not what you demand from it.

List 3: Ten Ways to Make Decisions That Protect the People You Lead

Count the cost to others before you count the benefit to yourself. — Every decision has a blast radius. Before you pull the trigger, ask: who absorbs the impact? Your wife? Your children? Your team? Your employees? A decision that benefits you at the expense of the people you lead is not leadership. It is exploitation with a good cover story.

Gather information before you gather opinions. — Opinions are cheap. Data is harder to find — and more valuable. Before you make a decision that affects other people, do your homework. Read the report. Check the numbers. Talk to the people closest to the problem. A leader who decides based on gut instinct alone is gambling with other people's lives. Instinct should confirm what the evidence already suggests.

Sleep on it when the pressure says decide now. — Urgency is rarely as urgent as it feels. The salesman says the deal expires tonight. The boss says he needs an answer by noon. The emotion says move right now. But most decisions — even the ones that feel like emergencies — can survive twenty-four hours of reflection. The decisions you will regret most are the ones you made in the heat of the moment. Sleep is the cheapest insurance policy a leader can buy.

Ask who is not in the room. — The people affected by your decision may not be the people sitting at the table. The employee who wasn't invited. The family member who doesn't know. The community that will feel the ripple. A good leader makes decisions with the voices in the room. A great leader makes decisions with the voices that aren't.

Consider the second and third consequences. — Every decision has a first consequence — the obvious one. But it also has a second and third — the ones you don't see until it's too late. If I take this job, what happens to my commute, my family time, my health? If I fire this person, what happens to the team, the morale, the workload? Think downstream. The best leaders are chess players, not checkers players.

Choose the harder right over the easier wrong. — The shortcut is always available. The compromise is always on the table. And the people you lead are always watching to see which one you choose. A leader who takes the harder right — even when the easier wrong would go unnoticed — builds a culture that outlasts him. Integrity at the decision point is the foundation of every culture worth building.

Communicate the decision and the reasoning. — People can accept a decision they disagree with if they understand why it was made. What they cannot accept is being blindsided by a choice they had no context for. Tell your team — or your family — what you decided and why. Not as a defense. As a respect. Because the people who follow you deserve to know where they're going and why.

Own the bad ones. — Not every decision will be right. Some will fail. Some will hurt people you were trying to protect. When that happens, own it. Publicly. Without hedging. "I made that call. It was wrong. Here's what I'm doing to fix it." A leader who owns bad decisions earns more trust than a leader who only claims the good ones.

Protect the vulnerable before the powerful. — In every decision, someone has more to lose. The employee with no savings. The child with no voice. The wife who depends on you. Lead with the most vulnerable person in mind, not the most influential. A decision that protects the strong at the expense of the weak is not leadership. It is cowardice.

Pray before you decide. — Not as a formality. As a lifeline. "God, show me what I can't see. Protect the people this decision will touch. Give me wisdom I don't have." A leader who prays before deciding is a leader who has acknowledged the limits of his own understanding — and has invited the only unlimited perspective into the room. That's not weakness. That's the wisest leadership move available.

List 4: Ten Ways to Admit You Were Wrong and Still Lead Forward

Say it plainly. — "I was wrong." Three words. No preamble. No softening. No corporate jargon. The power of a direct admission is that it clears the air instantly. Everyone in the room already knows you were wrong. The only question is whether you're willing to say it. When you do, the relief is audible — because a leader who can name his failure is a leader who can be trusted with the truth.

Don't explain it away. — The moment you follow "I was wrong" with "but here's why," you've taken back the admission. The explanation feels like a justification — and justification tells the room that you're still protecting yourself. If the context matters, share it later. In the moment of the admission, let the words stand alone. They are more powerful without a chaser.

Apologize to the people who were affected. — The admission is for you. The apology is for them. Look the person — or the team — in the eye and say, "I'm sorry for the impact this had on you." That sentence shifts the focus from your ego to their experience. And a leader who centers the affected rather than the accused is a leader worth following out of the wreckage.

Don't make the same mistake twice. — One mistake earns grace. The same mistake repeated earns doubt. The fastest way to prove that your admission was genuine is to demonstrate that the behavior has changed. Write it down. Build a safeguard. Ask someone to hold you accountable. A mistake that produces change is a lesson. A mistake that repeats itself is a pattern.

Ask for feedback on how you could have done it differently. — This is the part most leaders skip — and the part that matters most. "What did you see that I missed?" "How should I have handled this?" These questions are not signs of weakness. They are invitations for wisdom. And the team that is asked to contribute to the correction is the team that believes the correction is real.

Move forward with clarity and confidence. — Admitting you were wrong does not mean retreating. It means recalibrating. Once the admission is made and the apology is given, the leader's job is to stand up and say, "Here's what we do next." Dwelling in the mistake erodes confidence. Moving forward from it with a clear plan restores it.

Let it make you more careful, not more cautious.
— There is a difference. Careful means thoughtful, deliberate, informed. Cautious means afraid, hesitant, paralyzed. A mistake should sharpen your decision-making — not destroy it. The leader who stops deciding because he once decided wrong is no longer leading. He is hiding.

Don't bring it up repeatedly. — Once you've owned it, let it rest. A leader who keeps revisiting his own failures in public is not modeling humility — he is modeling insecurity. Acknowledge it. Learn from it. Then put it behind you. The team doesn't need to see you flagellate. They need to see you lead.

Use it to make space for others' mistakes. — A leader who has publicly failed and publicly owned it creates an environment where failure is survivable. Your team now knows: if the boss can be wrong and still lead, then I can be wrong and still belong. That psychological safety — born from your transparency — is one of the most valuable things a leader can build.

Remember that your credibility is not destroyed by one mistake — it's built by how you handle it. — The leaders history remembers are not the ones who never failed. They are the ones who failed, owned it, and came back stronger. Your wrong decision is not the end of your leadership story. It is the chapter that proves your character was tested — and held.

List 5: Ten Ways to Lead Under Pressure Without Breaking

Slow everything down. — Pressure compresses time. It makes everything feel urgent, immediate, irreversible. The first act of a leader under pressure is to resist that compression. Breathe. Pause. Speak more slowly than you feel. A leader who slows down in a crisis becomes the anchor everyone else grabs onto. Speed kills in combat and in decision-making.

Control your body first. — Before you manage the situation, manage yourself. Unclench your jaw. Drop your shoulders. Lower your voice. Open your hands. Your body tells the room what your words haven't said yet — and if your body says panic, the room will follow. Physical composure under pressure is not an act. It is a discipline. Train it.

Separate the facts from the fear. — Under pressure, the mind inflates. The mistake becomes a catastrophe. The delay becomes a disaster. The criticism becomes a death sentence. Step back and name what is actually true — not what feels true. "We missed a deadline" is a fact. "We're going to lose everything" is a fear. A leader who can distinguish between the two will make decisions that survive the moment.

Communicate more, not less. — When pressure hits, most leaders go silent. They retreat to figure it out, to process, to plan. But silence in a crisis breeds fear. Your team — your family — doesn't need the final answer. They need to hear your voice. "Here's what I know. Here's what I don't know yet. Here's what I'm doing about it." That alone is enough to stop the spiral.

Delegate what you don't have to carry. — You cannot carry everything. And the leader who tries to will collapse under the weight. Under pressure, identify what only you can do — and give the rest away. Not as abandonment. As trust. The people around you are capable of more than you think. Let them prove it. Your job under pressure is not to do everything. It is to direct everything.

Make the next right decision. — You don't need to solve the whole problem. You need to solve the next piece of it. Under pressure, the entire landscape can feel overwhelming — too many variables, too many unknowns. Ignore the whole landscape for a moment. Focus on the next step. What's the next right thing to do? Do that. Then do the next one. Sequential clarity is how leaders navigate chaos.

Stay close to the people who steady you. — Under pressure, isolation is the enemy. You need the friend who tells you the truth. The wife who brings perspective. The mentor who has survived worse. Don't retreat into yourself. Reach outward. The man who has people around him under pressure is the man who doesn't break under it.

Don't sacrifice the long term for the short term. — Pressure makes you think small — what will fix this right now? But the quick fix often creates a bigger problem tomorrow. The leader under pressure asks not just "What solves this today?" but "What does this decision look like in six months?" Short-term survival at the cost of long-term integrity is not leadership. It is panic.

Accept what you cannot control. — Some things under pressure are beyond your reach. The market. The other person's decision. The outcome of the diagnosis. A leader under pressure must identify, quickly and clearly, what he can control and what he cannot — and then pour every ounce of his energy into the former. Wrestling with the uncontrollable is not leadership. It is exhaustion.

Lean into your faith. — When the pressure exceeds your capacity — and it will — there is only one place to go. Not to another strategy. Not to another opinion. To the One who holds outcomes you cannot see. "God, I can't carry this. I need You." That prayer, spoken in the middle of the storm, is not a sign that the leader has broken. It is a sign that he knows where his strength actually comes from.

List 6: Ten Ways to Raise Up Other Leaders Instead of Building a Kingdom Around Yourself

Give away your best opportunities. — The project that would have made you look good — give it to the younger man who needs the experience. The speaking slot that would have boosted your profile — offer it to someone who's ready but hasn't been seen yet. A leader who hoards opportunities builds a career. A leader who gives them away builds a legacy.

Teach everything you know. — Don't protect your methods, your strategies, your secrets. Pour them into the people around you. The insecure leader withholds knowledge because he believes it makes him indispensable. The secure leader shares everything because he knows his value is not in what he knows — it's in who he builds.

Let them fail. — This is the hardest part of raising leaders. You see the mistake coming. You could step in and prevent it. But if you always catch them, they never learn to catch themselves. Let them stumble. Let them feel the weight of the consequence. Then be there — not to say "I told you so," but to say, "What did that teach you?" Failure, handled well, is the greatest leadership development tool in existence.

Celebrate their wins louder than your own. — When the person you mentored gets the promotion, make sure everyone knows how proud you are. When the leader you raised launches something successful, be the first to applaud. The secure leader finds joy in the success of others — because he knows that their success is the ultimate evidence that his leadership was real.

Push them into rooms they're not ready for. — Not to embarrass them. To stretch them. The meeting they think they can't handle. The conversation they're afraid of. The decision they've never made before. Growth happens at the edge of comfort, and a leader's job is to walk people to that edge — and then stand behind them, not in front of them.

Be honest about your own journey. — Tell them about the mistakes you made. The decisions you got wrong. The seasons that almost broke you. A leader who only shares his victories produces followers who are afraid to fail. A leader who shares his failures produces leaders who know that failure is not fatal.

Don't create dependency. — If your team cannot function without you, you haven't built leaders — you've built an audience. The goal is not a group of people who need you. The goal is a group of people who have become you — in integrity, in competence, in character. And when that happens, you should be able to walk away and watch them thrive. That's the finish line. Not applause. Independence.

Ask them what they think before you tell them what you think. — This simple act changes everything. Instead of broadcasting the answer, you invite them into the process. "What would you do here?" Their answer may surprise you. And even if it doesn't, the act of being asked builds a confidence in them that no instruction ever could. Leaders are built in the asking, not in the telling.

Invest disproportionately in the willing. — Not everyone wants to lead. Not everyone is ready. And your time is finite. Find the ones who are hungry — the ones who ask questions, who take initiative, who stay late not because they're told to but because they care. Pour into them. Not equally — disproportionately. A gallon of water on dry soil produces more than a gallon of water in a swamp.

Measure your leadership by what happens after you leave. — The true test of a leader is not what the organization looks like while he's there. It is what it looks like after he's gone. Did it grow? Did it sustain? Did the people he invested in become leaders themselves? If the answer is yes, then the man didn't just lead. He multiplied. And multiplication is the only form of leadership that outlives the leader.

List 7: Ten Ways to Stand Alone When the Crowd Goes the Other Way

Know what you believe before the pressure arrives. — A man who hasn't defined his convictions in peace will not find them in the storm. Decide now — before the room turns, before the culture shifts, before the consequences become real — what you stand for. Write it down. Rehearse it. Because when the moment comes, you will not have time to figure out what you believe. You'll only have time to act on it.

Accept that standing alone is the price of integrity. — No one will throw you a parade for doing the right thing when the right thing is unpopular. Standing alone is not glamorous. It is lonely, misunderstood, and often costly. But the alternative — joining the crowd you know is wrong just to avoid the discomfort — costs more. It costs your self-respect. And a man without self-respect has nothing left to lead with.

Don't mistake consensus for truth. — The majority can be wrong. History is littered with moments where the crowd moved in one direction and the truth stood in the other. Slavery was consensus. Silence during injustice was consensus. The fact that everyone agrees does not mean everyone is right. Truth is not determined by volume. It is determined by principle.

Be willing to lose the relationship to keep the conviction. — This is where it gets expensive. The friend who wants you to compromise. The boss who wants you to look the other way. The group that will drop you if you dissent. A man who stands alone must be prepared to stand without the people he stood beside. Not because the relationship doesn't matter — but because the conviction matters more.

Speak your position once, clearly, and then let it breathe. — You don't need to argue. You don't need to convince. You don't need to win. Say what you believe. Say it with respect. Say it without apology. And then let it sit. The truth doesn't need volume. It needs clarity. And the man who states his position once with conviction is more powerful than the man who repeats it a hundred times with desperation.

Don't demonize the people who disagree. — Standing alone does not mean standing in contempt. The crowd going the other way is full of people — some of them good, some of them confused, some of them afraid. You can disagree without dehumanizing. You can hold your position without hating theirs. The man who stands alone with grace is far more persuasive than the man who stands alone with arrogance.

Find the one other person. — Standing alone doesn't always mean standing literally alone. Sometimes there is one other person — one voice in the room who sees what you see. Find that person. Stand together. Even a minority of two is stronger than a minority of one. And that partnership, forged in resistance, will become one of the most meaningful relationships of your life.

Remember who you answer to. — At the end of the day, the crowd goes home. The boss goes home. The culture moves on to the next outrage. But you go home to your wife, your children, your mirror, and your God. And the question is not "Did they approve?" The question is "Did I do what was right?" If the answer is yes, the crowd's opinion is irrelevant.

Draw strength from the men who stood before you. — You are not the first man to stand alone. Others have stood where you stand — against tyranny, against corruption, against popular opinion, against the comfortable lie. Their stories are your fuel. Read them. Study them. Let their courage remind you that the men who stood alone were almost always the men history eventually thanked.

Understand that standing alone is temporary. — The crowd turns. Truth surfaces. Time reveals what the moment concealed. The man who stands alone today may be the man the world follows tomorrow — not because he changed, but because the world finally caught up. Stand firm. The loneliness is real, but it is not permanent. And what you're standing on will outlast what they're standing on.

List 8: Ten Ways to Lead with Integrity When Cutting Corners Would Be Easier

Do the full work. — The shortcut is always available. Skip the step. Fudge the number. File the report without double-checking. No one will know. But you will know. And a man who leads with integrity does the full work — not because someone is watching, but because the standard is the standard, regardless of the audience.

Charge what it's worth. — Don't inflate. Don't deceive. Don't pad the invoice, overstate the value, or exploit the customer's ignorance. Fair dealing is a form of leadership because it sets a tone that others follow. The man who charges honestly in a world of inflated prices stands out — and standing out for honesty is the best kind of marketing.

Tell the truth when the lie would go undetected. — This is the real test. Not when you'll be caught — but when you won't. The expense report no one audits. The résumé detail no one verifies. The conversation no one overheard. Integrity in the undetectable moments is the only integrity that counts. Everything else is compliance.

Refuse the deal that doesn't feel clean. — Trust your gut. If the opportunity requires you to look the other way, explain away a detail, or silence a question that keeps coming back — walk away. Clean money is better than fast money. And the deal you refused on principle will protect you from the consequences the man who took it will face later.

Keep the same standard when business is bad. — Integrity is easiest when the numbers are good. The real test is when the pipeline is dry, the bills are due, and the shortcut would solve the cash flow problem overnight. That's when integrity costs the most — and when it matters the most. The man who holds the line when the pressure is greatest is the man who can be trusted in every other season.

Pay people what you owe them, on time. — Vendors. Contractors. Employees. Partners. If you owe money, pay it. If you promised a timeline, meet it. Delayed payment is not a strategy — it is a statement about your character. And the people on the other end of that delay remember. They always remember.

Don't use people as stepping stones. — The networking culture teaches men to build relationships based on utility — what can this person do for me? An integrity-led leader builds relationships based on value — what can I offer this person? The difference is invisible at first. Over time, it becomes the difference between a leader people follow and a user people avoid.

Say no when saying yes would be dishonest. — "Can you deliver by Friday?" No, you can't. Say so. "Is this the best product?" No, it's the cheapest. Say so. A leader who says yes to everything is not agreeable — he is unreliable. And unreliable men eventually lose the trust that honest men spend their lives building.

Hold your team to the same standard you hold yourself. — Integrity cannot be optional. If you expect honesty from your team but tolerate your own exaggerations, the standard collapses. If you expect punctuality but arrive when it's convenient, the expectation becomes a joke. A leader's integrity is only as strong as his willingness to apply it to himself first.

Accept that integrity is expensive — and pay the price gladly. — You will lose deals. You will be passed over. You will watch men with lower standards climb faster. And it will burn. But the man who leads with integrity builds something that the man who cuts corners never will — a life that can withstand scrutiny. From anyone. At any time. And that peace is worth more than every shortcut you ever refused.

List 9: Ten Ways to Handle Power Without Letting It Handle You

Remember where you came from. — The man in the position of power was once the man in the folding chair. The mailroom. The apprenticeship. The first day when he knew nothing and had nothing. A man who remembers his beginning treats people differently than a man who has forgotten it. Memory is the antidote to arrogance.

Surround yourself with people who will tell you the truth. — Power creates a bubble. The higher you go, the fewer people will tell you what you need to hear. Most will tell you what you want to hear. Find the people who won't — and keep them close. They are not your critics. They are your lifeline. A leader who only hears applause will eventually lead off a cliff while everyone behind him claps.

Use your power to lift others, not to leverage them. — The question every man with power should ask daily is: "Am I using this position to help people or to help myself?" If the answer is the latter, the power has already corrupted something. Power is a tool — and

tools are defined by what they build. Build people.
Build opportunity. Build the table where others can sit.

Set limits on your own authority. — A man who has
unchecked power is a man who will eventually abuse it.
Not because he's evil — because he's human. Build
guardrails. Invite oversight. Give your wife, your board,
your team the authority to challenge you. The strongest
leaders are not the ones with the most power. They are
the ones who voluntarily limit it.

Be the last to eat. — In the military, officers eat last.
The principle is universal. A leader with power should
be the last to benefit from it. The last to take the raise.
The last to leave early. The last to take the easier path.
Power that serves itself is tyranny. Power that serves
others is leadership.

Don't punish dissent. — The man who disagrees with
you is not your enemy. He may be your greatest asset.
A leader who punishes pushback creates a culture of
silence — and a culture of silence is a culture that
cannot self-correct. Let people challenge your ideas.
Welcome it. Thank them for it. The leader who can be
questioned without retaliation is the leader worth
trusting with power.

Hold your power loosely. — Someday it will be taken
from you. The position will end. The title will change.
The authority will transfer. And who will you be then? A
man who holds power loosely is a man who knows that
his identity is not in the title. When it's gone, he is the
same man he was before. A man who grips power will
be destroyed when it slips.

Give people access to you. — The powerful often insulate. They build layers — assistants, gatekeepers, protocols — that separate them from the people they serve. Resist this. Keep the door open. Answer the email. Return the call. A leader who is accessible is a leader who is accountable. And accountability is the best protection against the corruption that power invites.

Watch how you treat people who can do nothing for you. — Power reveals character at its most naked when interacting with people who have no leverage. The intern. The waiter. The custodian. The man who is kind to the powerful and dismissive to the powerless is a man whose kindness is transactional. Let your power make you kinder, not more selective.

Lay it down before it lays you down. — Every season of power has an expiration date. The wisest leaders know when to step aside — not when they're forced to, but when the time is right. Leaving well is the final test of a leader. The man who exits with grace, who passes the torch instead of clutching it, who writes the final chapter with dignity — that man honored the power he was given.

List 10: Ten Ways to Serve the People You Lead Rather Than Use Them

Ask what they need, not what they can give you. — The user asks, "How can this person help me?" The servant asks, "How can I help this person?" It's a fundamental orientation — and the people around you can feel the difference immediately. When you lead from a posture of giving rather than extracting, the loyalty you receive is not forced. It is freely given — because it was freely earned.

Remove obstacles from their path. — Your job as a leader is not to stand at the front and demand results. It is to stand behind the people doing the work and clear the way. What's slowing them down? What tools do they need? What bureaucracy is in the way? A leader who removes obstacles is a leader who multiplies the capacity of everyone around him.

Give them your time, not your leftover time. — A meeting with an employee or a mentee should not be the thing that gets rescheduled every week. Give the people you lead your focused, undistracted, uninterrupted time. Close the laptop. Put the phone away. Look them in the eye. Your time is the clearest indicator of your priorities — and people know exactly where they rank.

Fight for their growth, even when it means losing them. — The best leaders develop people so well that they eventually outgrow the role. When that happens, a user tries to keep them. A servant celebrates them and helps them find what's next. Fighting for someone's growth — even when it costs you their presence — is one of the highest forms of leadership.

Protect them from unnecessary pressure. — Not from all pressure — some pressure is healthy. But from the pressure that comes from poor planning, unclear expectations, office politics, or your own disorganization. A leader who shields his team from the messes he created is a leader who understands that his job is to carry the weight — not to distribute it.

Acknowledge them publicly. — Say their name. In the meeting. In the email. In front of the client. "This was their work. This was their idea." Public acknowledgment costs you nothing and gives them everything. The leader who is generous with credit builds a team that is generous with effort.

Know their story. — Their spouse's name. Their child's health issue. The thing that keeps them up at night. The goal they're working toward. When you know someone's story, you lead them as a person — not as a function. And people who are led as persons give a quality of work that people led as functions never will.

Take the hit for them. — The client is angry. The board is frustrated. The blame is rolling downhill. Step in front of it. Absorb it. Protect the person behind you — especially when they made the mistake. You can correct them privately later. But in the moment, the leader stands in the line of fire so his team doesn't have to. That is service. And it is unforgettable.

Create a culture where failure is survivable. — If the people you lead are afraid to fail, they will stop trying. And an organization — or a family — that stops trying is an organization that has already died. Make it clear: mistakes will be made. They will be addressed. And then we will move on. A leader who creates safety around failure creates a team that is willing to take the risks that produce greatness.

Leave the place better than you found it. — Whether it's a department, a church, a company, or a household — the final measure of servant leadership is the condition of the thing when you hand it off. Did the people grow? Did the culture improve? Are the systems stronger? If the answer is yes, then you didn't just lead. You served. And service is the only form of leadership that leaves a mark worth remembering.

LEADERSHIP: QUOTES

"A leader is one who knows the way, goes the way, and shows the way." —John C. Maxwell

"The greatest among you shall be your servant." —Matthew 23:11

"Before you are a leader, success is all about growing yourself. When you become a leader, success is all about growing others." —Jack Welch

"Management is doing things right; leadership is doing the right things." —Peter Drucker

"Whoever wants to become great among you must be your servant, and whoever wants to be first must be slave of all." —Mark 10:43-44

"The task of leadership is not to put greatness into people, but to elicit it, for the greatness is there already." —John Buchan

"A genuine leader is not a searcher for consensus but a molder of consensus." —Martin Luther King Jr.

"If your actions inspire others to dream more, learn more, do more, and become more, you are a leader." —Attributed to John Quincy Adams

"Where there is no vision, the people perish." — Proverbs 29:18

"The price of greatness is responsibility." —Winston Churchill

---

LEADERSHIP: PUTTING IT INTO PRACTICE

This week, take ownership of one problem at work that isn't your fault. — Don't assign blame. Don't wait for someone else to step up. Just handle it. Observe how the people around you respond to a man who owns what he didn't cause.

Identify one person you lead and ask them: "What's one thing I could do better?" — Then listen without defending. The answer will cost your ego and strengthen your leadership. Write it down. Act on it.

Give credit publicly to someone on your team this week. — In a meeting, in an email, or in front of a client — name the person and name the contribution. Watch what it does to their confidence and to the culture.

Make one decision this week that prioritizes the long term over the short term. — Even if the short-term option is easier, more profitable, or more popular. Document why you chose the harder path. That documentation is your leadership journal.

Mentor one younger man this month. — Buy him coffee. Ask about his goals. Share one lesson from your own failures. You don't need a formal program. You need thirty minutes and the willingness to invest in someone who's behind you on the road.

The next time you're under pressure, pause for sixty seconds before responding. — One full minute. In that minute, lower your voice, unclench your jaw, and ask yourself: "What's the next right decision?" Then make it.

Audit your private and public behavior. — Are you the same man in both? Where are the gaps? Write down one area where your private life doesn't match your public image — and make a plan to close the gap this week.

Say "I was wrong" to someone this week — without adding "but." — A coworker. Your wife. Your child. Your team. Just the admission. Just the ownership. Observe how the relationship shifts when a leader is willing to be human.

Delegate one task you've been hoarding. — Give it to someone capable and let them run with it. Resist the urge to micromanage. Trust them. Your ability to release control is a direct measure of your confidence as a leader.

Before every major decision this week, pray. — Not a quick thought. A real conversation with God. "Show me what I can't see. Protect the people this will affect. Give me wisdom." Then decide. A leader who prays before deciding is a leader who leads from a source greater than himself.

CATEGORY 6

WORK & PROVISION

List 1: Ten Ways to Work Like It Matters Even When Nobody's Watching

Do the job right the first time. — Not because someone is checking. Because you are someone who does things right. Cutting corners when the boss isn't looking doesn't make you efficient — it makes you a man whose standard is dependent on surveillance. The man who does the job right every time, regardless of who's watching, is a man who has internalized excellence as identity, not performance.

Show up early and stay until the work is done. — Not to be seen. To be ready. The man who arrives before he's expected and leaves after the job is finished has communicated something without saying a word: this matters to me. In a world where most men are calculating the minimum required effort, the man who gives more than expected becomes irreplaceable.

Clean up after yourself. — The workspace you leave behind tells the world who you are when no one is looking. The mess in the break room. The tools left out. The email left unanswered. A man who cleans up after himself — literally and metaphorically — is a man who respects the space he occupies and the people who share it.

Do the tasks no one wants and do them well. — Every workplace has invisible work — the jobs that carry no recognition, no promotion potential, no applause. Filing. Cleaning. Organizing. Following up. The man who does these willingly, without complaint, and with the same energy he brings to the spotlight tasks, is the man whose character is not for sale.

Treat every task as if it carries your name. — Because it does. Whether it's a presentation to the board or a stack of boxes in the warehouse, the quality of your work is a direct reflection of the man who produced it. A man who gives his best only when the stakes are high has revealed that his standard is situational. Let every task carry your full effort — because every task carries your reputation.

Don't gossip about coworkers. — The break room is not a courtroom, and you are not the judge. When you talk about someone behind their back — their performance, their habits, their character — you are not building alliances. You are eroding your own credibility. A man who gossips is a man no one trusts with anything that matters. Keep your mouth shut and your work loud.

Be the person who follows through. — You said you'd send the email. You said you'd make the call. You said you'd have it by Friday. Did you? Follow-through is the rarest commodity in any workplace — and the man who delivers what he promises, without being reminded, rises faster than the man with twice his talent and half his reliability.

Work with integrity when the system rewards dishonesty. — Some workplaces reward the man who cuts corners, inflates numbers, and plays politics. You are not that man. Even if the system rewards dishonesty, your character is not determined by the system — it is determined by you. Work clean. Let the man who cheats get the short-term reward. You're playing a longer game — and the long game always wins.

Take pride in work that no one will ever see. — The report that gets filed and forgotten. The repair behind the wall. The preparation that makes someone else's presentation shine. A man who takes pride in invisible work is a man who understands that the audience for his effort is not his boss — it is his own integrity. And integrity doesn't need applause to stay alive.

Remember that your work is worship. — Whatever you do, work at it with all your heart, as if working for the Lord. That's not a platitude — it's a reorientation. When the work feels meaningless, when the boss is unjust, when the task is beneath you — you are not working for them. You are working as an act of obedience, discipline, and devotion. The man who works as worship never runs out of reasons to give his best.

List 2: Ten Ways to Provide for Your Family Without Losing Your Soul

Define provision beyond the paycheck. — Your family needs food on the table and a roof overhead. But they also need a father who is present at dinner and a husband who is awake on the weekend. Provision is not just financial — it is emotional, spiritual, and physical. A man who provides a six-figure income and an empty chair at the table has not provided. He has funded an absence.

Set a number and protect the margin. — Know what your family needs to live. Not to live lavishly — to live well. Then protect the margin between that number and the number your ambition tells you to chase. The gap between enough and more is where most men lose their families. Not because they're greedy — because they never defined the finish line.

Come home before you're empty. — If you give everything to the job and bring the scraps home, your family gets a hollow man — present in body, absent in everything else. Leave something in the tank. Your children don't need the version of you that the office already consumed. They need the version with energy enough to get on the floor, to ask the question, to stay awake during the movie.

Don't let the job define who you are. — You are not your title. You are not your salary. You are not your company's logo. If you were laid off tomorrow, you would still be a father, a husband, a man of faith, a friend. The man who lets his job define him will be destroyed when the job disappears — and jobs always disappear eventually.

Say no to the promotion that costs your family. — Not every opportunity is an advancement. Some promotions come with travel that takes you from your children, hours that steal your evenings, and stress that poisons your home. Before you say yes, count the cost — not in dollars, but in presence. The corner office means nothing if the people in your house forgot the sound of your voice.

Talk to your wife about money honestly. — Not just the good news. The debt. The fear. The pressure. Financial secrecy breeds resentment and anxiety. Financial honesty breeds partnership and trust. She doesn't need you to have it all figured out. She needs you to let her in. A marriage that shares the burden of provision is a marriage that survives the storms that break isolated men.

Work hard in season and rest hard out of season. — There are seasons that demand more — a startup, a project, a deadline. That's life. But seasons are supposed to end. The man who is always in a hard season is not dedicated. He is addicted. Know when to push and know when to stop. Rest is not laziness. It is the discipline that keeps hard work sustainable.

Don't chase someone else's standard of living. — The neighbor's car. The coworker's house. The life you see curated on a screen. None of it is yours to chase. The man who provides faithfully within his means is not a failure because another man has more. Contentment is not the enemy of provision. It is the guard that keeps provision from becoming obsession.

Build something that outlasts the paycheck. — A skill. A business. A trade. A reputation. A man who depends entirely on an employer for his livelihood has placed his family's security in someone else's hands.

Build something on the side — not out of greed, but out of stewardship. The man who has options provides a different kind of security than the man who has only one.

Let your children see you work — and see you rest. — They need to see the discipline. The early mornings. The effort. The sweat. But they also need to see you close the laptop. Turn off the phone. Sit on the porch with their mother. A child who sees only a working father learns that work is everything. A child who sees a father who works and rests learns that work is important — but it is not the whole story.

List 3: Ten Ways to Build a Reputation That Opens Doors You Never Knocked On

Be known for your reliability. — Do what you say. Every time. Without fail. In a world where most people overpromise and underdeliver, the man who simply does what he committed to becomes extraordinary by default. Reliability is not flashy. It's not viral. But it is the single trait that makes people think of you first when an opportunity arises.

Be kind to everyone, regardless of their position. — The receptionist you greeted warmly five years ago may become the hiring manager who remembers your name. The intern you mentored may become the CEO who calls you for a partnership. Kindness is not a strategy — but it functions like one, because people never forget how you made them feel.

Let your work speak louder than your words. — Stop announcing what you're going to do. Just do it. The man who talks about his plans is performing. The man who quietly executes them is building. And the builder — the man whose results are undeniable — never has to market himself. The work does the marketing.

Never burn a bridge. — The boss who frustrated you. The client who was difficult. The partner who didn't deliver. Leave every professional relationship with your integrity intact. You don't have to be friends. You have to be decent. The world is smaller than you think, and the man you torch today may be the man standing between you and the next opportunity tomorrow.

Be generous with your knowledge. — Share what you know. Teach what you've learned. Help the person who's three steps behind you. The man who hoards knowledge builds a small empire. The man who gives it away builds a reputation that travels rooms he's never entered. Generosity with knowledge is one of the fastest ways to be known as a man worth knowing.

Handle failure publicly with grace. — You will fail. Publicly. Visibly. The question is not whether it will happen — it's how you respond. The man who fails and blames, deflects, and disappears earns a reputation for fragility. The man who fails and owns it, learns from it, and moves forward earns a reputation that makes people trust him with bigger things. How you lose is more memorable than how you win.

Keep your personal life clean. — Your reputation is not built only at the office. It is built in your marriage, your neighborhood, your friendships, your social media presence, and the way you carry yourself on a Saturday night. The man whose personal life is a mess will eventually watch that mess seep into his professional life. Character is not compartmentalized. It is a single fabric — and one tear weakens the whole cloth.

Deliver more than expected. — The man who does exactly what was asked has met the standard. The man who does more than was asked has exceeded it — and exceeding the standard is what creates word-of-mouth. Over-delivery is the compound interest of reputation. It pays dividends long after the task is forgotten.

Be patient. — Reputation is not built in a quarter. It is built across decades. The man who is consistent for twenty years builds a name that no single achievement can match. Don't rush the process. Don't try to shortcut the timeline. Just show up, do the work, treat people right, and let time do what time does — reveal who you really are.

Live in a way that needs no defense. — The strongest reputation is the one that never has to be explained. When someone questions your character, the people who know you should be the ones who answer — not because you asked them to, but because your life made the case. That kind of reputation is not built by advertising. It is built by living.

List 4: Ten Ways to Handle a Job You Hate with a Character Worth Respecting

Show up fully anyway. — The alarm goes off. You don't want to go. Everything in you says this isn't where you belong. Get up anyway. Get dressed anyway. Show up anyway. A man's character is not revealed in the jobs he loves. It is revealed in the jobs he endures with excellence. The work may be beneath your ambition. It is never beneath your integrity.

Refuse to let the environment change your standard. — If the culture is lazy, stay disciplined. If the leadership is dishonest, stay clean. If the people around you have quit internally, keep showing up with effort. Your standard is not a product of your environment. It is a product of your character. And a man who holds his standard in a broken environment is a man who will carry that standard into every room he enters for the rest of his life.

Do the work as unto God, not as unto the boss. — When your boss doesn't notice, God does. When your effort goes unrecognized, your character is still being shaped. Reframe the work. You are not laboring for a paycheck or a promotion. You are laboring as an act of stewardship — and the One who sees in secret is the One who rewards in the open.

Use the time to sharpen yourself. — A job you hate is not a dead end — it is a classroom. What can you learn here that you couldn't learn in a job you loved? Patience. Endurance. Humility. How to lead from the bottom. How to serve without recognition. The man who uses a bad season to grow is the man who exits the season stronger than he entered it.

Don't poison the well. — Complaining is contagious — and destructive. The man who walks the hallways spreading negativity is not venting. He is infecting. If you hate the job, that's valid. But spreading that hatred to every coworker who will listen doesn't make the job better — it makes the environment worse. Keep your frustration between you, your wife, and your God.

Treat the people around you like they matter — because they do. — Your coworkers didn't choose this any more than you did. The receptionist. The line worker. The manager doing her best with bad instructions. These are human beings, and your hatred of the job does not give you permission to treat them with less than your full respect. A man who is kind in a miserable environment is a man whose kindness is real.

Make a plan to leave — and work the plan. — Hating your job is not a life sentence unless you refuse to move. Update the résumé. Learn the skill. Build the savings. Network with intention. A man who complains without planning is a man who has chosen comfort over courage. You are not stuck. You are deciding to stay. When you decide to go, go with a plan.

Don't take it home. — Your wife didn't create the problem. Your children didn't design the dysfunction. When you walk through the front door, leave the frustration in the car. Your family deserves the best of you — not the leftover rage of a bad day at a bad job. Compartmentalize the misery. Protect the peace of your home like it's the most important thing you have — because it is.

Be grateful for what it provides. — It pays the bills. It puts food on the table. It keeps the lights on while you build toward something better. Gratitude doesn't mean you love the job. It means you recognize that the job is serving a purpose — even if that purpose is temporary. A man who can be grateful in a season he hates is a man who will be trustworthy in the season he loves.

Leave it better than you found it. — When the day comes to walk away, leave clean. Leave relationships intact. Leave the workspace organized. Leave a reputation that makes people say, "He hated being here — but you'd never have known it by the way he worked." That's not acting. That's character. And character is the only thing you take with you when the badge is turned in.

List 5: Ten Ways to Be the Hardest Worker in the Room Without Making It Your Identity

Work hard because it's right, not because it defines you. — There's a difference between a man who works hard and a man who is his work. The first goes home at night and is a husband, a father, a friend. The second goes home and is still at the office — mentally, emotionally, spiritually. Hard work is a virtue. Workaholism is an addiction wearing a respectable outfit.

Never announce your effort. — The man who tells everyone how hard he works has traded the work for the applause. Let the results speak. Let the consistency speak. If you have to narrate your own effort, the effort has become a performance — and performances are for audiences, not for building a life.

Take the rest seriously. — A man who brags about never resting is not tough. He is burning a resource he cannot replace. Rest is not the opposite of hard work. It is the partner of hard work. The man who works six days and rests one follows a pattern as old as creation — and it exists for a reason. You are not a machine. Stop pretending.

Be present when you're home. — If your body is on the couch but your mind is in the spreadsheet, you are not home. Hard work means giving your full effort to the task at hand — and when the task is your family, the full effort is required. The man who is mentally at the office while sitting next to his wife has not left work. He has brought it into the one place it doesn't belong.

Know when the season is over. — There are seasons that demand everything — the launch, the deadline, the crisis. Those are real, and your family can endure them. But if every season is the urgent one, you haven't built a career. You've built a trap. Learn to recognize when the push is over and have the discipline to return to the rhythm your family needs.

Let someone else be the hardest worker sometimes. — If you can't handle being outworked, your identity is in the wrong place. A man whose sense of self requires being the best in the room is a man who will crumble the day someone better walks in. Work hard because it's who you are — not because it's how you prove your worth.

Don't measure your day by your output alone. — Did you produce? Good. Did you also call your mother? Did you also listen to your son? Did you also sit with your wife without an agenda? The man who measures his day only by what he accomplished has forgotten that some of the most important things in life produce no measurable output at all.

Invest in hobbies that have nothing to do with productivity. — Read a novel. Play an instrument. Walk in the woods. Build something with your hands that no one will ever buy. A man who cannot enjoy something unless it's productive has confused living with performing. Your worth is not a function of your output. It never was.

Ask your wife if you're giving too much to work. — She sees it before you do. She feels the absence before you notice it. Ask her — honestly — whether the balance is right. And when she tells you the truth, don't get defensive. Adjust. The man who asks and adjusts is the man whose family still recognizes him in ten years.

Die with people at your bedside, not projects. — No man's gravestone reads, "He answered every email." No eulogy celebrates a man's productivity metrics. The people you worked for will replace you. The people you loved will not. Work hard. Work honestly. Work with excellence. Then close the laptop, walk into the next room, and invest in the things that will actually be there at the end.

List 6: Ten Ways to Deal with Failure at Work Without Letting It Follow You Home

Name it before it names you. — You failed. Say it. Out loud if you have to. Not to shame yourself — to take ownership. The man who refuses to name his failure will spend weeks carrying it underground, where it festers into shame, anxiety, and self-destruction. Name it, examine it, and strip it of the power it holds when it lives in the dark.

Separate the failure from your identity. — You are not the project that fell apart. You are not the deal that collapsed. You are not the quarter that missed the target. You are a man who experienced a failure — and there is a universe of difference between those two sentences. Failure is an event. It is not a diagnosis. The man who treats it like a diagnosis will spend years recovering from something that should have taken months.

Debrief with honesty, not with blame. — What went wrong? What did you miss? What would you do differently? Answer these questions with the ruthless honesty of a man who wants to learn — not with the defensiveness of a man who wants to protect his image. The debrief is where the failure becomes tuition. Skip it, and you've paid the cost without getting the education.

Talk to one person about it. — Not everyone. Not the internet. One person you trust — your wife, your friend, your mentor. Say, "I failed at this, and it's eating me." The weight of a failure carried alone doubles every night. The weight of a failure spoken to a trusted person is halved the moment the words leave your mouth.

Don't replay the tape. — Your mind will want to loop the failure — the moment it went wrong, the thing you should have said, the decision you wish you could reverse. Every replay deepens the groove. Every loop adds weight. At some point, you have to press stop. Not because the failure doesn't matter — but because the replay is doing more damage than the failure itself.

Leave it at the threshold. — When you walk through your front door, the failure stays outside. Your children don't need a defeated father at the table. Your wife doesn't need a man who brings the office disaster into the bedroom. You can process it later. You can grieve it tomorrow. But right now, in this house, you are a husband and a father — and those roles don't answer to your quarterly numbers.

Get back to work the next day. — Not with manufactured enthusiasm. With discipline. The man who gets knocked down and gets back up the next morning — showing up on time, doing the work, refusing to let the failure become his posture — that man is building something the failure can't touch. Resilience is not the absence of defeat. It is the presence of the next step.

Find one thing you did well inside the failure. — Not to spin it. To calibrate. Even in the wreckage, something held. A decision you made correctly. A relationship you protected. A principle you didn't compromise. Find it. Hold it. It is the evidence that the failure did not consume you entirely — and that the man who walks forward has something to build on.

Refuse to let it make you timid. — The worst consequence of failure is not the loss — it's the fear that follows. The fear of trying again. The fear of deciding. The fear of putting yourself on the line. That fear, if you let it, will shrink your life to a size that feels safe but produces nothing. Take the next risk. Make the next decision. The man who fails and tries again is infinitely more dangerous than the man who never fails because he never tries.

Remember that every man you admire has a failure story. — The mentor who seems invincible? He failed. The CEO whose name you respect? He lost. The father you look up to? He made decisions he'd give anything to take back. Failure is not the disqualifier the world tells you it is. It is the prerequisite. No man who has ever built something meaningful did it without first losing something painful.

List 7: Ten Ways to Treat Money as a Tool and Not a Trophy

Stop measuring your worth by your bank account. — The world has built a scoreboard that counts dollars, and most men are playing by its rules without ever questioning them. Your worth as a man — as a father, a husband, a friend, a child of God — has never been determined by a number. The man with millions who neglects his family is poorer than the man with little who sits at the table every night.

Give before you feel ready. — Generosity is not something you do after you've reached a comfortable surplus. It is something you do in the middle of the tension — when the budget is tight and the giving still costs you something. A man who waits until he's wealthy to give will find that wealth only deepens the grip. Give now. Give first. Give while it still stings. That's where the freedom lives.

Budget like a man who takes stewardship seriously. — Money without a plan is money without a master. And money without a master becomes the master. A budget is not a restriction — it is a declaration of priorities. It says, "This is what matters to me, and I will direct my resources accordingly." The man who budgets is not the man who has less. He is the man who controls more.

Teach your children that money serves — it does not rule. — If your children see you anxious over money, controlled by money, or obsessed with money, they will inherit the same prison. Show them what it looks like to earn honestly, give generously, save wisely, and hold loosely. Money should be a tool in your hand — never a chain around your neck. Teach them the difference while they're young enough to believe it.

Don't spend money you don't have to impress people you don't know. — The new car on a loan. The vacation on a credit card. The clothes you can't afford. Every purchase made to manage someone else's perception is a purchase that weakens your foundation. Impressions are temporary. Debt is persistent. The man who lives within his means has a freedom that the man financing a lifestyle will never know.

Know the difference between price and value. — The most expensive option is not always the best. The cheapest is not always the wisest. A man who treats money as a tool evaluates every expenditure by what it produces — for his family, his future, his faith, his community. Value is not a number. It is an outcome. Spend toward outcomes that matter.

Save like something unexpected is coming — because it is. — The job loss. The medical bill. The car that dies. The roof that leaks. A man who saves is not pessimistic — he is prepared. An emergency fund is not a luxury for the wealthy. It is a necessity for the faithful. The man who prepares for the storm while the sun is shining protects his family from the panic that destroys unprepared men.

Eliminate the debt and refuse to go back. — Debt is a leash. It limits your decisions, steals your options, and keeps you tethered to jobs you hate and lifestyles you can't sustain. Attack it. Sacrifice for it. Pay it off like your freedom depends on it — because it does. And once it's gone, guard the door. The man who escapes debt and returns to it has freed himself only to walk back into the cell.

Be transparent with your wife about every dollar. — No hidden accounts. No secret purchases. No financial decisions made without her knowledge. Money in a marriage is shared — and shared money requires shared visibility. The man who is transparent about finances builds trust. The man who hides them builds a time bomb.

Hold it all with open hands. — Everything you have was given to you. Your health. Your ability. Your opportunity. Your earnings. None of it is permanently yours — it is entrusted to you for a season. The man who holds money with open hands is a man who can give freely, lose gracefully, and live without the anxiety that comes from clutching something he was never meant to own.

List 8: Ten Ways to Mentor a Younger Man in Your Workplace

See him before he sees himself. — Most young men don't know what they're capable of. They're too close to their own insecurity to see their potential. That's your job. See the skill he hasn't developed. See the character that's forming. See the leader he could become if someone believed in him enough to say it out loud. One sentence from a man he respects can redirect his entire trajectory.

Invite him in. — To the meeting. To the project. To the conversation. Don't wait for him to ask — he won't. Young men are terrified of overstepping, and they'd rather stay invisible than risk looking presumptuous. You have to extend the invitation. "Come sit in on this."

"I want you in the room for this one." Those words open doors he didn't even know existed.

Be honest about your own failures. — If you only share your wins, he'll think leadership is a straight line. It's not. Tell him about the project you bombed. The relationship you mismanaged. The season you almost quit. Your honesty gives him permission to fail — and permission to fail is the single most important thing a mentor can give.

Teach him the things nobody teaches. — How to write a professional email. How to handle a difficult conversation with a boss. How to manage his first real paycheck. How to read a room. How to speak up without overstepping. These are the invisible skills — the ones that separate the men who advance from the men who stall. They're not in any textbook. They're in you.

Hold him accountable without hovering. — Give him a task. Set the expectation. Then step back and let him deliver. Check in, but don't micromanage. If he falls short, address it directly and kindly. If he delivers, acknowledge it. The goal is not to create a dependent — it is to build a man who functions with excellence when no one is standing over him.

Listen to his ideas without dismissing them. — He may be young. He may be inexperienced. He may suggest something you tried ten years ago and abandoned. Listen anyway. Not every idea will be good — but every idea deserves a hearing. The young man who is listened to becomes the man who speaks up. The one who is dismissed learns to stay silent. And silent men don't lead.

Challenge him beyond his comfort zone. — Give him the assignment that stretches him. The presentation he's not sure he can deliver. The client he's nervous to call. The responsibility that feels too big. Growth lives at the edge of comfort, and your job as a mentor is to walk him to that edge — and then stand close enough to catch him if he falls.

Protect him from the politics. — Every workplace has them — the games, the alliances, the unwritten rules that can destroy a career before it starts. Shield him where you can. Warn him where you can't. Teach him to navigate without compromising. A young man who learns early to stay clean in dirty water has been given a gift that will serve him for decades.

Don't take credit for his growth. — When he succeeds, resist the temptation to claim it. The mentor who says, "I made him what he is" has made the mentoring about himself. The mentor who says, "He did the work — I just opened a few doors" has made the mentoring about the man it was supposed to be about. Let his success be his own. That's the whole point.

Stay in his life after the job ends. — Mentoring doesn't expire when one of you changes companies. The best mentors are the ones who remain — a phone call away, a text away, a coffee meeting away — long after the workplace connection has ended. The relationship you built was never about the job. It was about the man. And the man is still becoming.

List 9: Ten Ways to Start Over When Everything You Built Falls Apart

Grieve what you lost. — The business. The career. The reputation. The years of work. Before you rebuild, let yourself feel the weight of what's gone. Grief is not weakness — it is the acknowledgment that something mattered to you, and it's been taken. A man who skips the grief and rushes to the rebuild will carry unresolved pain into the next structure — and pain makes a terrible foundation.

Take inventory of what survived. — You lost the job. But you still have your wife. You lost the business. But you still have your health. You lost the income. But you still have your integrity. The man who focuses only on what's gone will miss what's still standing. And what's still standing is what you'll rebuild from. Name it. Count it. Thank God for it.

Resist the temptation to blame. — The economy. The partner. The boss. The market. Some of those may have played a role — but the man who starts over by pointing fingers is a man who hasn't fully owned his part. And the man who hasn't owned his part will repeat the same patterns in the next venture. Take responsibility for what was yours. Leave the rest with God.

Start smaller than your pride wants. — The man who built a company doesn't want to go back to the entry-level position. The man who led a team doesn't want to sweep the floor. But starting over rarely means starting where you left off. It often means starting at the bottom — again. And the man who is willing to start small is the man who will build something bigger than what he lost.

Tell the people who matter. — Don't carry the collapse alone. Tell your wife. Tell your brother. Tell your mentor. Not because they can fix it, but because secrecy in failure is the breeding ground for shame. And shame immobilizes. It tells you to hide, to pretend, to withdraw. The antidote is honesty — and honest men rebuild faster than isolated ones.

Learn the lesson before you repeat the effort. — What went wrong? Not the circumstantial explanation — the real one. Did you grow too fast? Did you ignore advice? Did you cut a corner that mattered? Did you neglect the relationships that held the structure together? A man who starts over without learning the lesson is a man who is building the same house on the same cracked foundation.

Get your hands dirty immediately. — Don't sit in the rubble too long. Grief has a season — and then action must follow. Apply for the job. Register the business. Make the phone call. Start the plan. Movement is the enemy of despair. And the man who starts moving — even in the wrong direction — will find his way faster than the man who sits still and waits for clarity to arrive.

Rebuild your habits before you rebuild your income. — Before you chase the next dollar, rebuild the disciplines that will sustain you: prayer, exercise, budgeting, presence with your family, sleep, reading. These are the scaffolding that holds a life together while the structure is being rebuilt. Skip them, and the new structure will collapse under the same weight as the last one.

Accept help without shame. — The friend who offers money. The church that offers a meal. The neighbor who offers work. Accept it. Not as charity — as community. The man who refuses help because his pride won't allow it is not strong. He is isolated. And isolated men don't rebuild. They break.

Believe that what comes next can be better than what was lost. — Not as a cliché. As a conviction. Some of the greatest chapters in the lives of great men were written after the worst chapters ended. Loss clears the ground. Pain sharpens the vision. And the man who walks forward after the collapse — wiser, humbler, leaner, closer to God — is a man whose second act may be the one that defines him.

List 10: Ten Ways to Leave a Workplace Better Than You Found It

Train the person behind you. — Don't leave your replacement guessing. Write the notes. Record the processes. Sit with them. Answer the questions they're afraid to ask. The man who invests in his successor is a man who understands that the work was never about him — it was about the mission. And the mission continues after you're gone.

Thank the people who made your work possible. — The assistant who organized your calendar. The colleague who covered for you. The janitor who kept the lights on. Before you walk out the door, look those people in the eye and say, "Thank you." Not in an email. In person. Gratitude at the exit is a measure of a man's character — and the people who receive it never forget it.

Finish what you started. — Don't leave loose ends. Close the project. File the report. Return the call. A man who walks away mid-task has told the world that his convenience matters more than his commitment. Finish the work. Even if the next chapter is already calling. Completion is a discipline — and disciplined men leave clean exits.

Don't badmouth the company on your way out. — You may have legitimate grievances. The culture may have been broken. The leadership may have been poor. That's fine — but the exit interview is not the courtroom, and the break room is not the confessional. Leave with your dignity intact. The man who torches the bridge reveals more about himself than about the company.

Leave your workspace clean. — Empty the drawer. Wipe the desk. Remove your personal items. Return what isn't yours. The condition of the space you leave behind is a final signature — one that says either "I cared about this place" or "I couldn't wait to leave." Let your last impression be as strong as your first.

Repair the relationships you damaged. — If you wronged someone — a harsh word, a missed commitment, a broken trust — own it before you go. A brief, honest apology delivered on the way out can heal a wound that would otherwise live in that person's memory for years. You may not get another chance. Take this one.

Recommend someone else for the opportunities you're leaving. — You know who's ready. You've seen the talent, the character, the work ethic. Before you go, put their name in front of the people who make decisions. Advocacy from a departing colleague carries weight — and the man who lifts others on his way out has left the most valuable thing behind: a pathway.

Document what you learned. — Not just for your successor — for yourself. What skills did you build here? What mistakes did you make? What would you do differently? Write it down. A man who leaves without reflection has wasted half the experience. The other half was the paycheck. The real value was the lesson.

Send one final note to the person who invested in you most. — The manager who took a chance on you. The colleague who covered your weaknesses. The mentor who pulled you aside when you were struggling. Write them a note — handwritten if you can — and tell them what they meant to you. That letter will sit in their desk long after you've gone. And it will matter more than any exit survey ever could.

Walk out the door with your head high and your conscience clean. — No stolen supplies. No deleted files. No hidden resentment. No unpaid debts. Leave with the same integrity you walked in with — or more. The final chapter of your time at any workplace is not written by the company. It is written by you. Make it one that would make your children proud if they could read it.

WORK & PROVISION: QUOTES

"Whatever you do, work at it with all your heart, as working for the Lord, not for human masters." — Colossians 3:23

"The only way to do great work is to love what you do." —Steve Jobs

"A good name is more desirable than great riches; to be esteemed is better than silver or gold." —Proverbs 22:1

"The man who does not work for the love of work but only for money is not likely to make money nor to find much fun in life." —Charles M. Schwab

"For even when we were with you, we gave you this rule: 'The one who is unwilling to work shall not eat.'" —2 Thessalonians 3:10

"Do not wear yourself out to get rich; do not trust your own cleverness. Cast but a glance at riches, and they are gone, for they will surely sprout wings and fly off to the sky like an eagle." —Proverbs 23:4-5

"Far and away the best prize that life offers is the chance to work hard at work worth doing." —Theodore Roosevelt

"Lazy hands make for poverty, but diligent hands bring wealth." —Proverbs 10:4

"Success is not final, failure is not fatal: it is the courage to continue that counts." —Attributed to Winston Churchill

"Commit to the Lord whatever you do, and he will establish your plans." —Proverbs 16:3

WORK & PROVISION: PUTTING IT INTO PRACTICE

This week, arrive fifteen minutes early to work every day. — Not to impress anyone. To set the tone for the day before the day sets the tone for you. Use the quiet to prepare, to pray, to prioritize. Watch how it changes the trajectory of your mornings.

Ask your wife this question: "Am I giving too much to work and not enough to us?" — Listen to her answer without defending yourself. She sees the imbalance before you feel it. Whatever she says, adjust. The correction is a gift.

Identify one younger man at work and invest in him this month. — Buy him coffee. Ask about his goals. Share one lesson you've learned the hard way. Thirty minutes of mentoring can redirect a man's entire career.

Look at your family's budget and find one area where you're spending to impress rather than to provide. — The subscription you don't use. The upgrade you don't need. The purchase you made because someone else had one. Cut it. Redirect the money toward savings or giving.

Write down three things your job has taught you that have nothing to do with the job itself. — Patience. Perseverance. Humility. Conflict resolution.

Whatever it is — name it. Even a job you hate is shaping you into someone. Make sure you know who.

This week, do one task at work that no one asked you to do and no one will see. — Clean the break room. Organize the shared drive. Help the new employee find their footing. Invisible work builds invisible character — and invisible character is the only kind that lasts.

Turn off all work notifications from 6 p.m. to 6 a.m. for one full week. — The work will survive without your 10 p.m. email check. Your family will notice the difference immediately. And you'll discover that the urgent rarely is.

If you're in debt, write the total number on a piece of paper and tape it to your bathroom mirror. — Not to shame yourself. To face it. Every morning, look at the number and recommit to the plan. Debt thrives in denial. It dies in daylight.

Before you leave your current job — whether it's tomorrow or in ten years — write a one-page document of everything you've learned there. — Lessons, relationships, mistakes, skills. This is your exit portfolio. It's worth more than any reference letter because it proves you paid attention.

Pray over your work this week. — Before the meeting. Before the difficult conversation. Before the first email. Ask God to use your hands, your mind, and your integrity to honor Him in the work He's placed before you. Then work like a man who believes He's watching — because He is.

CATEGORY 7

PHYSICAL DISCIPLINE

List 1: Ten Ways to Train Your Body Like a Man Who Respects the Gift

Stop treating exercise as optional. — It is not a hobby. It is not a phase. It is not something you do when you feel motivated. It is a responsibility — to your wife, your children, your future self, and the God who gave you the body you're neglecting. The man who treats his body as optional will one day find out that the body he ignored has become a prison he cannot escape.

Move every single day. — Not every day needs to be a gym day. Some days it's a walk. Some days it's a stretch. Some days it's twenty minutes of something that makes your heart pound and your lungs burn. The point is movement — consistent, daily, non-negotiable. A body in motion stays capable. A body at rest decays. Choose which one you want to be at sixty.

Train for longevity, not for vanity. — The mirror is a liar. It tells you that the goal is aesthetics — the arms, the chest, the number on the scale. The truth is that the goal is decades. Can you pick up your grandchild? Can you climb the stairs at seventy? Can you carry your wife's groceries at eighty? Train for the long game. The man who trains for the mirror will quit when the mirror stops cooperating. The man who trains for his future never runs out of reasons.

Lift heavy things. — Muscle is not decoration. It is infrastructure. It holds your skeleton together, protects your joints, keeps your metabolism working, and gives you the physical capacity to do the things life demands. You do not need a gym membership to lift heavy things. You need a willingness to push your body against resistance — and the discipline to do it regularly.

Learn to be uncomfortable on purpose. — Hard runs. The last rep you didn't think you could finish. The hill you wanted to walk but ran instead. Physical discipline is the practice of choosing discomfort before life forces it on you. And the man who has practiced discomfort in the gym will handle the discomfort that arrives at his doorstep far better than the man who has spent his life avoiding it.

Stop making excuses about your age. — You are not too old to start. You are not too far gone to improve. Men decades older than you are running marathons, lifting weights, and living with a vitality that would embarrass half the men in their thirties. Age is a factor — not a sentence. Adjust the intensity. Modify the movement. But never stop. The man who uses age as his excuse has chosen to age faster.

Train with other men. — Accountability multiplies discipline. Find a partner. Join a group. Show up at the same time and push each other. A man who trains alone will eventually quit when motivation fades. A man who trains with brothers will show up because someone is expecting him — and that expectation is the difference between consistency and collapse.

Respect the recovery. — Rest days are not weakness. They are the days your body rebuilds what you broke. Sleep is not laziness. It is the single most important recovery tool you have. A man who trains hard and rests well will outperform the man who trains every day and sleeps five hours. Your body is not a machine. Stop running it like one.

Track your progress. — What gets measured gets managed. Write down what you lifted, how far you ran, how many reps you completed. Not for the internet — for yourself. Progress is often invisible to the eye but undeniable on the page. And on the days when you feel like you're going nowhere, the record will show you how far you've come.

Remember whose body it is. — You did not make yourself. Your heart beats without your permission. Your lungs fill without your effort. Your body was given to you — entrusted to you — and one day you will give an account for how you stewarded it. That is not guilt. It is gravity. Treat the gift with the seriousness it deserves.

List 2: Ten Ways to Build Discipline That Lasts Beyond the Gym

Start with the alarm clock. — Discipline begins the moment the alarm sounds. Not when you feel like it — when the clock says so. The man who gets up when he doesn't want to has already won the first battle of the day. And the first battle sets the tone for every battle that follows.

Make the bed. — It takes sixty seconds. It produces zero applause. And it is one of the most reliable discipline builders known to man. A made bed is a completed task before the day has started — a small act of order in a world that trends toward chaos.

Eat with intention, not with impulse. — Discipline at the table is discipline everywhere. The man who eats whatever is in front of him, whenever he feels like it, without thought or restraint, is the same man who will struggle with impulse in every other area of his life. Plan your meals. Eat to fuel, not to numb.

Keep your word on the small things. — You told your wife you'd take out the trash. You told your friend you'd call him back. You told yourself you'd read before bed instead of scrolling. These are not grand commitments. They are the bricks of discipline — and the man who keeps his word on the small things builds the muscle to keep his word on the ones that matter most.

Set a time to stop consuming content. — The screen is the single greatest enemy of modern discipline. It promises five minutes and steals two hours. It promises relaxation and delivers numbness. Set a hard stop — a time each night when the device goes away and the man who was hiding behind it comes back to life.

Do the hardest thing first. — Every day has a task you're dreading — the call, the conversation, the workout, the report. Do it first. Not after coffee. Not after you've warmed up to the day. First. The man who does the hardest thing first has removed the weight that would have hung over the rest of his day.

Build routines that don't require motivation. — Motivation is a guest. It shows up, stays for a while, and leaves without notice. Discipline is a resident. It lives in routines — the morning routine, the workout routine, the evening routine — that happen regardless of how you feel. The man who waits for motivation will live an inconsistent life. The man who builds routines will outlast every motivated man in the room.

Fast from something regularly. — Not just food. Comfort. Entertainment. Social media. The act of voluntarily going without something you enjoy builds a muscle that most modern men have never trained — the muscle of self-denial. And self-denial, practiced regularly, produces a man who is not controlled by his appetites. He controls them.

Finish what you start. — The book you opened. The project you began. The commitment you made. Discipline is not the enthusiasm to start — it is the resolve to finish. And the man who finishes what he starts, even when the excitement has worn off, is the man who builds a life of substance rather than a trail of half-completed intentions.

Hold yourself to a standard higher than what's required. — The minimum is someone else's standard. Yours should be higher. Clean the kitchen better than it needs to be. Finish the report earlier than it's due. Run the extra mile no one asked for. A man who exceeds the standard in private will exceed it in every arena he enters. Discipline is not about doing what's expected. It's about doing what's excellent.

List 3: Ten Ways to Eat Like You Give a Damn About Your Future

Stop eating like a teenager. — The metabolism that forgave you at twenty will betray you at forty. The fast food, the late-night binges, the meals that come from a window — those aren't sustaining you. They're slowly dismantling you.

Cook your own food. — A man who can feed himself is a man who controls what goes into his body. Learn to grill a piece of meat. Learn to roast vegetables. Learn to make a meal that doesn't come from a box or a bag. Cooking is not beneath you. It is one of the most practical forms of self-sufficiency a man can possess.

Eat at the table. — Not in front of the screen. Not in the car. Not standing over the counter. Sit down. Use a plate. Eat slowly. When you eat at the table — especially with your family — you are not just nourishing your body. You are practicing presence.

Drink water like your life depends on it — because it does. — Before the coffee. Between the meals. After the workout. The simplest health intervention available to any man is drinking enough water — and most men don't do it.

Stop using food as a reward. — You had a hard day. You earned it. You deserve the extra plate, the dessert, the late-night run to the drive-through. That voice is a liar. Food is fuel. The moment it becomes your emotional regulation strategy, you've handed your body over to your feelings — and feelings make terrible nutritionists.

Read the label. — You don't need a degree in nutrition. You need the discipline to turn the package over and read what's in it. If the ingredient list looks like a chemistry experiment, put it back. A man who reads labels is a man who has decided to stop outsourcing his health to companies that profit from his ignorance.

Eat more plants than you think you need. — This is not a political statement. It is a biological one. Your body needs fiber, vitamins, and nutrients that no amount of protein powder can replace. Add the vegetables. Eat the fruit. Build the salad.

Plan your meals before the hunger decides for you. — Hunger is impulsive. It doesn't care about your goals. The man who plans his meals in advance has removed hunger from the decision-making process. Preparation is not obsessive. It is strategic.

Eat less than you think you need. — Most men eat more than their bodies require — not out of hunger, but out of habit, boredom, or emotional need. Push back from the table slightly before you're full. The man who practices restraint at the table practices restraint everywhere.

Teach your children to eat well by eating well yourself. — They are watching. If you eat garbage, they will eat garbage. But if you sit down, eat real food, drink water, and talk about why it matters — they will carry that discipline into their own kitchens, their own families, and their own futures. Your plate is their curriculum.

List 4: Ten Ways to Rest Without Guilt and Work Without Burnout

Accept that rest is a commandment, not a suggestion. — God Himself rested. Not because He was tired — because He was establishing a pattern. Six days of work. One day of rest. The man who ignores it is not tougher than God. He is more arrogant.

Sleep like it's medicine — because it is. — Seven to eight hours. Non-negotiable. Sleep rebuilds your muscles, consolidates your memory, regulates your emotions, and strengthens your immune system. The man who brags about sleeping four hours a night is not disciplined. He is deteriorating in slow motion.

Take one full day off every week. — Not a half day where you check email after lunch. A full day. No work. No obligations that drain you. The man who cannot take a day off is not dedicated. He is addicted.

Stop glorifying exhaustion. — "I'm so busy." "I haven't slept in two days." "I'm running on fumes." These are not badges of honor. They are symptoms of a man who has lost control of his schedule.

Schedule your rest the same way you schedule your work. — If it's not on the calendar, it won't happen. Block the Saturday afternoon nap. Block the

Sunday without plans. Rest that is vague will always lose to work that is scheduled.

Learn to do nothing. — Sit on the porch. Watch the sky. Let your mind wander. Do not reach for the device. Doing nothing is not wasted time. It is the space where creativity breathes, where problems solve themselves, and where the soul catches up with the body.

Take the vacation. — Not the working vacation where you answer emails by the pool. The real vacation — where you leave the laptop at home and give your family the version of you that has nowhere else to be.

Say no to the thing that will cost you your peace. — The extra commitment. The weekend project. The favor that isn't really a favor. Every yes is a no to something else — and too often, the something else is your rest, your family, your health.

Pay attention to the warning signs. — Irritability. Insomnia. Loss of appetite. Withdrawal from the people you love. Cynicism about the work you used to enjoy. These are the body's alarm system telling you that the pace is unsustainable.

Rest as an act of trust. — When you rest, you are saying, "God, I trust that the world will not fall apart while I stop." That is a profound statement of faith — because the man who cannot rest is the man who believes that everything depends on him. It doesn't.

List 5: Ten Ways to Break an Addiction That's Been Breaking You

Call it what it is. — Not a habit. Not a preference. An addiction. The alcohol. The pornography. The substance. The screen. Whatever has its hands around your throat — name it. Out loud. Naming it strips it of the anonymity that lets it thrive.

Stop believing you can manage it alone. — You've tried. You've white-knuckled it. You've made it a week, maybe two, and then you're back. That pattern is not a failure of willpower. It is evidence that willpower alone is not enough. You need help — a counselor, a group, a brother.

Identify the trigger before the fall. — Every addiction has a pattern. Stress leads to the drink. Loneliness leads to the screen. Boredom leads to the scroll. Learn the chain — the feeling that precedes the behavior — and interrupt it before it completes.

Remove the access. — If the bottle is in the house, you will drink it. If the screen is unlocked at midnight, you will use it. Remove the access. Pour it out. Install the filter. Delete the account. Give your wife the password. These are not extreme measures. They are the minimum measures required for a man who is serious about his freedom.

Replace the addiction with something that builds you. — The addiction filled a void — boredom, pain, loneliness, stress. If you remove the addiction without filling the void, the void will pull you back. Replace the drink with the workout. Replace the screen with the book. Replace the isolation with the brotherhood.

Tell one person everything. — Not the sanitized version. The whole truth. How long it's been going on. How deep it goes. What it's cost you. The power of addiction lives in secrecy. Sunlight is the disinfectant.

Expect the withdrawal to be brutal — and endure it anyway. — The first week will be the hardest thing you've ever done. Your body will scream for the thing you took away. Your mind will negotiate. Your emotions will lie to you. Endure it. The discomfort is not a sign that you're failing. It is a sign that the chains are breaking.

Forgive yourself for yesterday and fight for today. — You will relapse. Probably more than once. And the shame of the relapse is the most dangerous moment — because shame whispers, "See? You can't change." That voice is a liar. Forgive yourself. Get up. Fight again.

Build accountability that is regular and specific. — Not a vague check-in. A specific, weekly conversation with a man who asks the hard questions. "Have you used this week? Have you been honest with your wife? Have you been alone with the thing that's killing you?"

Let God into the wound. — The addiction is the symptom. Beneath it is a wound — rejection, trauma, fear, grief, emptiness. And that wound will not heal under your own power. Let God into the place you've been medicating. The deepest healing is not behavioral. It is spiritual. And the man who lets God touch the wound is the man who walks free.

List 6: Ten Ways to Age Strong Instead of Just Getting Old

Move every day like your independence depends on it — because it does. — The man who stops moving at fifty will be immobile at seventy. The man who keeps walking, stretching, lifting, and bending will be carrying his grandchild at eighty. Movement is not about the gym. It is about freedom.

Protect your joints. — Your knees, your shoulders, your hips, your back — these are the hinges of your independence. Stretch them. Strengthen the muscles around them. Stop ignoring the pain that keeps coming back.

Keep your mind sharp. — Read. Learn. Solve problems. Have conversations that challenge your thinking. The brain, like the body, atrophies when it's not used. Stay curious. Stay engaged.

Maintain your friendships. — Isolation is one of the leading killers of aging men. Keep the friendships alive. Make new ones. Show up at the table. Call the man you haven't spoken to in months. Connection is not a luxury. It is a lifeline.

Get the checkup. — The blood work. The physical. The screening. The test you've been avoiding. Catch the problem early. Know your numbers. The fifteen minutes you spend in a doctor's office could buy you fifteen years with your family.

Eat like a man who wants to be here in twenty years. — The metabolism slows. The tolerance narrows. What you could eat at thirty will destroy you at sixty. Adjust. More vegetables. Less sugar. More water. Less alcohol.

Sleep like you mean it. — Sleep becomes harder with age — and more important. Protect the sleep. Darken the room. Put the screen away an hour before bed. Your body is rebuilding itself while you sleep. Give it the time to finish the job.

Stay useful. — Purpose keeps men alive. The man who retires from work and retires from usefulness will fade faster than anyone expects. Volunteer. Mentor. Build something. Teach something. A man with something to do tomorrow has a reason to wake up in the morning.

Carry your own weight. — Carry the groceries. Mow the lawn. Shovel the driveway. Do as much as you can for as long as you can. Independence is a muscle that must be used or it disappears.

Prepare for the end with the same discipline you brought to the beginning. — Get the will in order. Have the conversations. Tell the people you love what they mean to you. The man who prepares for his death is not morbid — he is responsible.

List 7: Ten Ways to Stop Treating Your Body Like It's Disposable

Admit that you've been negligent. — Not as self-flagellation. As a starting point. You've eaten what was easy. You've skipped what was hard. You've numbed what hurt instead of healing it. Acknowledge it. Not with shame. With honesty.

Stop waiting for the crisis to change. — Most men don't change until the doctor says a word that terrifies them. Don't wait for the alarm. Change now — while the runway is still long enough to correct course.

Quit the thing that's killing you. — You know what it is. The cigarettes. The nightly drinking. The fast food every day. The energy drinks replacing sleep. Quitting is hard. Not quitting is harder — it just delays the consequences.

Move your body like you owe it something — because you do. — It carried you through every season of your life. It healed your broken bones. It got you through the nights you didn't think you'd survive. Start moving. Not to punish yourself — to honor the machine that has never stopped working for you.

Sleep like it's the most important thing you do — because on most days, it is. — Your muscles recover during sleep. Your brain cleans itself during sleep. Your hormones regulate during sleep. And yet most men treat sleep like a negotiable line item. Stop. Go to bed.

Drink less. — Not a popular sentence. But a necessary one. Alcohol is a toxin your liver has to process. You don't have to quit. But you have to be honest about how much you're consuming — and whether that number serves your future or sabotages it.

Get outside. — Sunlight. Fresh air. The sound of something that isn't a notification. Your body was designed to exist in the natural world. Walk outside. Stand in the sun. Breathe air that hasn't been filtered through a building.

Stretch. — Your muscles are shortening. Your posture is curving. Your range of motion is shrinking. Stretch every day. It takes ten minutes. It costs nothing. And it is the difference between a body that moves with ease at sixty and a body that has become a cage.

See the doctor before you see the emergency room. — Preventive care is not cowardice. It is wisdom. The man who goes in for a checkup catches the problem at stage one. The man who waits catches it at stage four.

Treat your body as a trust, not a toy. — It does not belong to you alone. It belongs to the wife who sleeps beside you. The children who need you at their graduation. The grandchildren who should know your voice. Every decision you make about your body is a decision you're making about theirs.

List 8: Ten Ways to Build Endurance for the Long Fights in Life

Train the body to endure discomfort. — The run that makes your lungs burn. The set that makes your muscles scream. These are not punishments. They are rehearsals. The man who has trained his body to push through physical discomfort will find that emotional and spiritual discomfort becomes more survivable.

Develop a morning routine that doesn't negotiate with feelings. — The alarm. The prayer. The movement. The reading. Every day. Not when you feel like it — when the clock says so. A morning routine anchored to the clock rather than the mood produces a man who is not governed by what he feels.

Practice patience in the small frustrations. — The traffic. The slow line. The delayed flight. The child who asks the same question six times. These are the training ground for your endurance. The man who loses his temper in traffic will lose his composure in the crisis.

Stay in the hard conversation. — When your wife brings the topic you've been avoiding. When your friend challenges you on the thing you don't want to face. Stay. Endurance is not just physical. It is the capacity to remain emotionally present when everything in you wants to leave.

Commit to something that takes years, not weeks. — A marriage. A faith journey. A physical transformation. The culture of instant results has trained men to expect fast returns — and to quit when the returns don't come. Endurance is forged in long commitments.

Study the men who endured. — Read about the men who survived prison camps, who walked through deserts, who rebuilt after total loss. Their stories are fuel. Not because your struggle is the same, but because their endurance proves it's possible.

Stop quitting when it stops being fun. — Marriage stops being exciting. Work stops being new. Exercise stops being motivating. These are not signs that something is wrong. They are signs that you've entered the stage where endurance is required. The deepest

rewards in life are not at the beginning. They're at the
end.

Build rest into the endurance, not after it. —
Endurance is not the refusal to rest. It is the discipline
to rest strategically so that you can keep going. The
marathon runner who sprints the first mile collapses
before the finish. The one who paces himself crosses
the line.

Let your faith carry what your strength cannot. —
There will come a season when your body is tired, your
mind is exhausted, and your emotions have nothing
left. In that season, endurance is not a human
achievement. It is a spiritual one. The man who
endures beyond his own capacity has accessed a
strength that is not his own.

Remember why you started. — In the middle of the
long fight — when the end is nowhere in sight — go
back to the beginning. Why did you start? Who are you
fighting for? That answer is your fuel. Write it down.
Read it when the tank is empty.

List 9: Ten Ways to Show Up Physically for the People Who Depend on You

Be the man who can carry the load. — The furniture
that needs moving. The child who needs lifting. The
bag that's too heavy for her. These are not chores. They
are opportunities to be useful, to be present, and to be
the man your family looks to when something physical
needs to happen.

Be the one who walks them to the car at night. — Not because the world is always dangerous. Because your presence communicates something that no security system can replicate: I am here. I am watching. You are safe with me.

Play with your children. — Get on the floor. Chase them in the yard. Throw them in the air. Wrestle on the living room carpet. Your children do not need a father who watches from the sideline. They need a father whose body is in the game.

Be physically capable in a crisis. — Know CPR. Know how to stop bleeding. Know how to lift someone who's fallen. Know how to carry a child out of a building. The crisis will not wait for you to look up the instructions.

Stay strong enough to protect. — You do not need to be a fighter. But you need to be capable — capable of standing between your family and a threat, capable of moving quickly when urgency demands it. Physical strength is not aggression. It is insurance.

Don't let fatigue become your excuse. — Your daughter wants you to push her on the swing. Your son wants to throw the ball. Your wife wants to take a walk after dinner. And you're tired. But the man who says, "Not tonight" every night is the man whose family stops asking. Get up. Be tired and present.

Take care of the house. — Fix the leak. Mow the grass. Change the light bulb. Paint the room she's been asking about. A man who lets his home fall apart has communicated, without words, that the space his family occupies is not worth his effort.

Drive with care. — The most common physical danger your family faces is the car ride. Put the phone away. Watch the road. Slow down. A man who drives recklessly with his family in the car has failed the most basic physical responsibility he has.

Show up healthy. — Not perfect. Healthy. Be the man whose family doesn't worry about losing him to a heart attack at fifty-five. Your health is not just yours. It belongs to everyone who loves you.

Be the last to sit down and the first to stand up. — When there's work to be done, be the man on his feet. When someone needs help, be the man already moving. That decision, lived out daily, is what makes a man irreplaceable.

List 10: Ten Ways to Compete with Yourself Instead of Comparing Yourself to Others

Measure yesterday against today. — The only competition that matters is the one between who you were and who you are becoming. Did you move more today than yesterday? Did you eat better this week than last? That's your scoreboard. Every other man's progress is irrelevant to your race.

Delete the content that makes you feel inferior. — The transformation video. The highlight reel. The man with the perfect body selling you his program. These are designed to make you feel inadequate so that you'll buy what he's selling. Remove the input. Your competition is not the man on the screen.

Celebrate the small win. — You held the plank ten seconds longer. You ate clean for three days straight. You went to bed on time. These are victories. Celebrate them. Because the man who celebrates small wins builds the momentum to chase the big ones.

Set goals based on your capacity, not someone else's. — If you can run a mile, don't compare yourself to the man running ten. Run a mile. Then run a mile and a half. Progress is personal.

Track your own data. — Reps. Miles. Weight. Sleep. Water. Whatever you're building — measure it. Not for the internet. For yourself. The record of your own progress is more motivating than any comparison could ever be.

Compete in effort, not in outcome. — You can control how hard you work. You cannot control the result. The man who gives his absolute best — regardless of where he finishes — has won the only race that matters.

Be inspired by other men without being threatened by them. — The man who is stronger than you is not your enemy. He is your evidence — evidence that more is possible. Let his discipline inspire yours. But do not let his existence diminish yours.

Compete against your excuses. — The weather. The schedule. The fatigue. The mood. Your greatest opponent is not another man. It is the voice inside your head that says, "Not today." Beat that voice.

Forgive yourself for the setback. — You missed a week. You ate badly. You skipped the workout. Fine. Forgive yourself. Don't quit. The man who stumbles and gets back up is not a failure. The man who stumbles and stays down is.

Remember that the goal is not to be the best. — The goal is to be better. Better than you were last month. Better than the version of you that quit. You don't need to be the strongest man in the room. You need to be stronger than you were yesterday. That's enough. That's always been enough.

PHYSICAL DISCIPLINE: QUOTES

"Do you not know that your bodies are temples of the Holy Spirit, who is in you, whom you have received from God? You are not your own; you were bought at a price. Therefore honor God with your bodies." —1 Corinthians 6:19-20

"No man has the right to be an amateur in the matter of physical training. It is a shame for a man to grow old without seeing the beauty and strength of which his body is capable." —Socrates

"Discipline is the bridge between goals and accomplishment." —Jim Rohn

"Take care of your body. It's the only place you have to live." —Jim Rohn

"Physical fitness is not only one of the most important keys to a healthy body, it is the basis of dynamic and creative intellectual activity." —John F. Kennedy

"I discipline my body and keep it under control, lest after preaching to others I myself should be disqualified." —1 Corinthians 9:27

"The last three or four reps is what makes the muscle grow. This area of pain divides a champion from someone who is not a champion." —Arnold Schwarzenegger

"Endure hardship as discipline; God is treating you as his children." —Hebrews 12:7

"Strength does not come from physical capacity. It comes from an indomitable will." —Mahatma Gandhi

"The body achieves what the mind believes." —Author Unknown

PHYSICAL DISCIPLINE: PUTTING IT INTO PRACTICE

Move your body for thirty minutes every day this week. — Walk, run, lift, stretch — whatever fits your level. No excuses. No negotiation. Thirty minutes. Build the habit before you build the program.

Set your alarm thirty minutes earlier tomorrow and get up when it sounds. — Not ten more minutes. Not after you scroll. When it rings, your feet hit the floor. That one act of discipline will change the posture of your entire day.

Replace one meal this week with something you cooked yourself. — Not from a box. Not from a drive-through. Real food, prepared by your own hands. The act of feeding yourself intentionally is a declaration of ownership over your own health.

Put the screen down one hour before bed for seven consecutive nights. — Read a book. Talk to your wife. Sit in silence. Let your brain wind down without the artificial stimulation that's been stealing your sleep for years.

Drink a full glass of water before every meal this week. — Before the coffee, before the food, before anything else. Hydration is the simplest discipline available to you — and the one most men neglect first.

If you have an addiction, tell one person the truth this week. — Not the whole world. One person. Say the words out loud: "I'm struggling with this." The weight you've been carrying alone will halve the moment it's shared.

Schedule a doctor's appointment this month. — The physical. The blood work. The screening. Whatever you've been putting off. Do it this month. Your family needs you alive more than they need you tough.

Find one man to train with and commit to a weekly session. — Not a professional. A friend. A brother. A man who will show up and push you and expect you to do the same.

Fast from one comfort this week. — Sugar. Alcohol. Social media. The snack you reach for out of habit, not hunger. Go without it for seven days. Not to punish yourself — to prove to yourself that you are in control.

At the end of each day this week, write down one physical thing you did to honor your body. — The workout. The healthy meal. The walk. The glass of water. The rest. Build a record of care. After seven days, read it back. You are building something.

CATEGORY 8

MENTAL TOUGHNESS

List 1: Ten Ways to Endure Pain Without Becoming Bitter

Acknowledge the pain instead of burying it. — The man who says "I'm fine" when he's breaking is not tough. He's terrified. Toughness is not the denial of pain. It is the willingness to name it — to say, "This hurts. This is real. And I'm going to carry it without letting it carry me." The man who buries pain doesn't eliminate it. He gives it a place to grow in the dark — and what grows in the dark eventually surfaces in ways he cannot predict or control.

Refuse to let the wound become your identity. — What happened to you matters. It shaped you. It scarred you. But it is not you. The man who builds his identity around his wound becomes a man who cannot function without it. He introduces himself by his trauma, filters every relationship through his suffering, and makes the pain the center of everything. That's not endurance. That's captivity. You are not what happened to you. You are what you do next.

Separate the person from the pain they caused. — This is one of the hardest disciplines in existence. The boss who fired you unjustly. The father who abandoned you. The friend who betrayed you. The human being and the action are two different things. You can

condemn the action without condemning the person —
and when you do, the bitterness loses its grip.
Bitterness requires a villain. Remove the villain, and all
you're left with is a wound — and wounds, unlike
villains, can heal.

**Choose the story you tell yourself about what
happened.** — You can tell yourself a story of
victimhood — "The world is against me. People can't be
trusted. Nothing good ever lasts." Or you can tell
yourself a story of refining — "This broke me open. It
forced me to grow. It made me a man I couldn't have
become without it." Both stories are available. Only one
leads somewhere worth going. The man who chooses
the refining story doesn't deny the pain. He redeems it.

Stop rehearsing the offense. — Every time you
replay the moment — the words, the betrayal, the loss
— you are re-injuring yourself. You are reopening the
wound with your own hands and then wondering why it
won't heal. At some point, the replay has to stop. Not
because the offense was small. Because your future is
bigger than your past, and you cannot walk forward
while staring backward.

Find meaning in the suffering. — Not forced
meaning. Not toxic positivity. But the honest
recognition that pain, endured well, produces
something that comfort never could. Empathy. Depth.
Compassion. The ability to sit with another man in his
darkest hour and say, "I know," and mean it. A man
who has suffered well becomes a sanctuary for men
who are suffering now. And that is not a consolation
prize. That is a calling.

Refuse to punish the innocent for the guilty. — Your wife didn't hurt you — your ex did. Your children didn't betray you — your partner did. Your new friend didn't let you down — the old one did. Bitterness is contagious. It leaks into every relationship, poisoning the ones that had nothing to do with the original wound. The man who contains the bitterness to its source protects the people who love him from a fire they didn't start.

Pray for the person who hurt you. — This is the nuclear option against bitterness — and the one most men refuse to deploy. Pray for their family. Pray for their peace. Pray for their growth. It will feel impossible at first. It will feel dishonest. Do it anyway. Because bitterness cannot survive in a heart that is genuinely praying for the person it wants to hate. Something breaks. Something shifts. And the man who started the prayer angry finishes it free.

Serve someone whose pain is greater than yours. — Bitterness thrives in isolation and self-focus. It withers in the presence of service. Volunteer at the shelter. Visit the hospital. Sit with the dying. When you place your pain next to someone else's and choose to serve them, your pain doesn't disappear — it repositions. It becomes smaller. Not because it wasn't real, but because perspective has entered the room.

Give it time and stop demanding instant resolution. — Some pain takes years to process. Some grief revisits in waves. Some wounds scar over slowly, then reopen on the anniversary, the birthday, the holiday. That's not weakness. That's human. Give yourself the grace to heal at the pace that healing

requires — and resist the temptation to call yourself
bitter just because you're still hurting. Healing and
bitterness are not the same thing. The difference is
direction. If you're still moving forward, you're healing.
If you've set up camp in the pain, that's bitterness.
Keep moving.

List 2: Ten Ways to Control Your Emotions Before They Control You

Recognize the feeling before the reaction. — Anger
doesn't arrive without a signal. It starts in the chest,
the jaw, the fists. Sadness starts in the throat. Anxiety
starts in the stomach. Learn your body's language. The
man who can feel the emotion rising before it reaches
his mouth is the man who has a choice — and choice is
the entire difference between a man who controls
himself and a man who is controlled.

**Create space between the stimulus and the
response.** — Something happens. Someone says
something. The impulse is immediate — fire back, shut
down, escalate, withdraw. But between the thing that
happened and the thing you do about it, there is a gap.
A fraction of a second. And in that gap lives your
freedom. The man who learns to widen that gap —
through a breath, a pause, a deliberate silence — is the
man who never has to apologize for what he said in the
heat of the moment.

Name the emotion out loud. — "I'm angry right
now." "I'm afraid." "I'm hurt." The simple act of
naming the emotion reduces its power. It moves the

feeling from the limbic brain — where it's chaotic and reactive — to the prefrontal cortex, where it can be examined. You cannot manage what you cannot name. And the man who can say, "I'm furious right now, and I need a minute," has just done something most men never learn to do.

Separate the emotion from the decision. — Emotions are information. They are not instructions. You can feel angry and still speak kindly. You can feel afraid and still act bravely. You can feel sad and still show up for your family. The emotion tells you something is happening. It does not tell you what to do about it. The man who lets the emotion make the decision is the man who spends his life cleaning up after his feelings.

Stop using anger as your default setting. — Men are trained to convert every emotion into anger because anger feels powerful. Sadness feels exposed. Fear feels weak. Grief feels unmanageable. So the mind routes everything through the one channel that feels masculine — rage. But beneath the anger is almost always something softer and truer. Hurt. Disappointment. Fear. The man who can bypass the anger and reach the real emotion underneath it is the man who actually resolves things instead of just escalating them.

Walk away before the damage is done. — Not as a retreat. As a strategy. "I need to step out for ten minutes." That sentence has saved more marriages, friendships, and careers than any piece of advice ever written. The man who walks away before the explosion is not running. He is choosing to protect the people in the room — including himself — from words that cannot be unsaid.

Journal what you feel. — Not for the internet. For yourself. Write down the anger, the fear, the grief, the confusion. Get it out of your head and onto a page. Something happens when a man translates his emotions into words on paper — they become smaller, more manageable, more visible. The page holds what the mind cannot. And a man who writes his way through his emotions is a man who doesn't drown in them.

Exercise the emotion out of your body. — When the anger is boiling or the anxiety is climbing, move. Run. Lift. Walk hard and fast. Emotions are not just mental events — they are physical ones. Your body stores what your mind cannot process. And the fastest way to discharge an emotion that is overwhelming your system is to move your body until the chemistry shifts. It's not avoidance. It is regulation.

Ask yourself what you'd tell your son. — If your son came to you with the same anger, the same heartbreak, the same frustration — what would you tell him? Would you tell him to scream? To punch the wall? To shut down? Or would you tell him to breathe, to think, to respond with control? Whatever you would tell him is what you need to tell yourself. Be the man you're trying to raise.

Surrender what you cannot control. — Half of your emotional turmoil comes from trying to control things that were never in your hands. Other people's opinions. The outcome of the meeting. The behavior of your teenager. The economy. The diagnosis. When you surrender what you cannot control and focus entirely on what you can — your response, your character, your next step — the emotional noise drops dramatically. Not because the situation changed. But because you stopped fighting a war you were never meant to win.

List 3: Ten Ways to Stay Focused When Everything Around You Is Noise

Decide what matters before the day decides for you. — If you don't define your priorities before the morning starts, the morning will define them for you — and its priorities are notifications, obligations, other people's emergencies, and the endless pull of the feed. Write down three things that matter today. Do those first. Everything else is secondary.

Turn off the noise — literally. — The notifications. The background chatter. The news cycle on repeat. The podcast you don't need. The music that fills every silence. Some of it is harmless. Much of it is stealing your ability to think. A man who cannot sit in a quiet room cannot focus in a noisy one. Train in the silence so you can perform in the chaos.

Limit your inputs. — You are consuming more information in a single day than your grandfather consumed in a month. Most of it is noise dressed as news, opinion dressed as fact, and content designed to hold your attention, not improve your life. Curate ruthlessly. Unfollow. Unsubscribe. Delete. The man who controls his inputs controls his focus.

Do one thing at a time. — Multitasking is a myth.
What you're actually doing is switching between tasks
rapidly — and every switch costs focus, energy, and
quality. When you're writing, write. When you're
talking, talk. When you're with your children, be with
your children. The man who does one thing at a time
does everything better than the man who does
everything at once.

Build a morning routine that anchors you. —
Before the inbox, before the scroll, before the noise of
the world rushes in — anchor yourself. Prayer.
Movement. Reading. Writing. The first hour of your day
sets the trajectory for the remaining fifteen. A man who
starts his day in someone else's agenda will spend the
rest of it chasing. A man who starts in his own will
spend it leading.

Protect your peak hours. — You have two to four
hours each day when your mind is sharpest. Most men
waste those hours on email, meetings, and
administrative tasks that require no creativity. Identify
your peak hours and guard them like gold. Do the deep
work — the writing, the strategizing, the building —
when your brain is at its best. Do the shallow work
when it's not.

Say no more often. — Every yes is a no to something
else. And most men say yes to things that are urgent
but unimportant while saying no — by default — to
things that are important but not urgent. Your family.
Your health. Your deep work. Your faith. Learn to say
no to the good so you can say yes to the essential.
Focus is not the ability to do more. It is the discipline to
do less.

Schedule blocks of uninterrupted time. — Two hours with no meetings, no messages, no knocks on the door. Block it on the calendar. Defend it. The most valuable work you'll ever do requires sustained concentration — and sustained concentration requires the absence of interruption. If your days are chopped into thirty-minute fragments, you are busy but not productive.

Stop checking. — The email. The message. The feed. The score. The notification. Every check breaks your focus and costs you ten to fifteen minutes of reentry time. And if you check twenty times a day, you've lost hours to a habit that produces nothing. Set a time to check — twice a day — and ignore it the rest of the time. Your focus will triple.

Remember what you're building. — Focus without purpose is just discipline for discipline's sake. But focus in service of a vision — a marriage, a family, a book, a business, a legacy — is unstoppable. The man who knows what he's building can resist any distraction. The man who doesn't know will be distracted by everything. Clarity of purpose is the ultimate filter. Get clear. Then stay focused.

List 4: Ten Ways to Handle Rejection Like a Man Who Knows His Value

Let it sting — but don't let it stay. — Rejection hurts. That's not a flaw. That's proof that you cared enough to put yourself out there. Feel the sting. Acknowledge the disappointment. But set a time limit on the wallowing. The man who feels the pain and moves through it is fundamentally different from the man who sets up camp inside it.

Don't let one person's no rewrite your entire narrative. — The publisher said no. The employer said no. The woman said no. That is one data point — not a verdict on your worth. The man who lets a single rejection define him has given one person more power than they deserve. Your value was never dependent on their answer.

Separate the rejection from your identity. — They rejected the pitch. Not the man. They passed on the application. Not the person. The moment you fuse the rejection to your sense of self, you've taken something external and made it internal — and internal wounds are the hardest to heal. Keep the distance. What they said no to was a moment. You are a lifetime.

Ask what you can learn — then move. — Was there something in your approach that could improve? Was the timing wrong? Was the fit off? Learn the lesson. Write it down. Then close the notebook and move forward. The man who learns from rejection gets better. The man who relives it gets stuck.

Don't broadcast it for sympathy. — The temptation after rejection is to go public — to vent on a screen, to tell every friend, to turn your disappointment into content. Resist. Process it privately. Share it with one or two people you trust. The man who broadcasts his rejection is looking for validation. The man who processes it quietly is looking for growth.

Remember every door that opened before this one closed. — You've been accepted before. You've been chosen before. You've been wanted, needed, affirmed, and valued. One closed door doesn't erase the hallway of open ones behind it. The man who fixates on the no forgets the history of yeses that brought him to where he stands.

Keep swinging. — The job didn't come through. Apply again. The relationship ended. Stay open. The venture failed. Start another. The most successful men in history were not the ones who avoided rejection. They were the ones who absorbed it and kept moving. Persistence in the face of rejection is not stubbornness. It is faith — faith that the right door hasn't been reached yet.

Don't punish the next opportunity for the last one's failure. — The man who was burned by one employer doesn't give his best at the next job. The man who was rejected by one woman builds walls against the next. This is how rejection wins — not by what it does to you in the moment, but by what it convinces you to withhold in the future. Don't let yesterday's no steal tomorrow's yes.

Surround yourself with men who remind you who you are. — After a rejection, the voice in your head gets loud — and it lies. "You're not good enough. You'll never make it. Who do you think you are?" You need a friend who will look you in the eye and say, "That's not true. I know who you are. Get back up." One sentence from a brother can silence the voice that rejection amplified.

Root your value in something rejection cannot touch. — If your worth is built on achievement, every rejection shakes the foundation. If your worth is built on approval, every no dismantles it. But if your worth is rooted in something deeper — in your identity as a man created by God, loved by God, purposed by God — then rejection becomes a surface event. It stings. It doesn't destroy. Because the deepest part of you was never on the table.

List 5: Ten Ways to Think Clearly Under Pressure

Breathe first. — It sounds absurdly simple. It is also absurdly effective. When pressure hits, the body constricts — breath shortens, muscles tighten, vision narrows. One deep breath — slow in, slow out — interrupts the cascade. It tells the nervous system to stand down. And a man who can breathe before he reacts is a man who can think before he speaks.

Ask what is actually true right now. — Pressure amplifies. It turns a setback into a catastrophe. A challenge into an impossibility. A risk into a certainty of failure. The antidote is to ask, flatly and without emotion: what is actually true right now? Not what might happen. Not what could go wrong. What is true at this moment? That question alone cuts the noise in half.

Reduce the decision to its simplest form. — Under pressure, everything feels complex. But most decisions, when stripped of emotion and assumption, come down to a simple binary. Do I stay or go? Do I speak or wait? Do I act or hold? Simplify the decision. The man who can reduce complexity under pressure is the man who moves while others freeze.

Remove the audience from your mind. — Half the pressure you feel isn't from the problem — it's from the people you imagine watching you solve it. Your boss. Your wife. Your team. Your father. Their imagined judgment magnifies the stakes. Remove them from the equation. What would you do if no one were watching? That's usually the clearest answer.

Write it down. — When the mind is spinning, the pen stops the spin. Write the problem on a piece of paper. Write the options. Write the worst-case scenario and the best-case scenario. Seeing it on paper shrinks it. The mind inflates. The page contains. And the man who can externalize the chaos can finally think inside the calm.

Slow your speech. — Under pressure, the mouth speeds up. Words tumble out unfiltered, emotional, reactive. Slow down. Speak half as fast as you feel. The act of slowing your speech forces your brain to think ahead of your mouth — and thinking ahead of your mouth is the entire point. Calm speech produces calm thinking. Rapid speech produces regret.

Recall a time you survived something worse. — You've been here before — or somewhere close. And you survived. That memory is not nostalgia. It is evidence. Evidence that you have the capacity to handle what's in front of you because you've handled things before that felt just as impossible. The man who remembers his past endurance is the man who trusts his present capacity.

Focus on the next step, not the whole staircase. — The full scope of the problem is overwhelming. The entire plan is too much to hold. So don't hold it. Hold the next step. What is the single next right thing to do? Do that. Then ask again. The man who moves one step at a time under pressure will climb the staircase. The man who stares at the top will never start.

Consult someone calmer than you. — You are inside the storm. You need someone who is outside it. A mentor. A wife. A friend. Someone who can see the situation without the emotion you've attached to it. "Here's what I'm facing — what do you see?" That question has rescued more decisions than any amount of solitary analysis.

Pray — not for escape, but for clarity. — "God, I can't see straight right now. Clear my mind. Show me the next step. Give me the wisdom I don't have." That prayer, spoken under pressure, does something no strategy can replicate — it connects you to a source of clarity that is not limited by your emotions, your fatigue, or your fear. Pray first. Think second. Act third.

List 6: Ten Ways to Rebuild Your Mind After Trauma or Loss

Accept that you are not the man you were before. — The loss changed you. The trauma rewired something. You will not go back to who you were — and trying to will only deepen the frustration. The goal is

not restoration. It is reconstruction. You are building a
new version of yourself — one that carries the scar but
is not defined by it. That man can be stronger. But he
will be different.

Let the grief come in waves without fighting it. —
It will hit you in the car. In the shower. At 3 a.m. On a
Tuesday afternoon when nothing triggered it. Don't
resist it. Let it come. Let it wash over you and recede.
Fighting grief doesn't make it stop. It makes it louder.
The man who surrenders to the wave — without
drowning in it — is the man who heals.

Talk to someone who is trained to help. — Not just
a friend. A counselor. A therapist. A professional who
understands trauma and can guide you through the
reconstruction. This is not weakness. This is the same
wisdom that sends a broken bone to a surgeon instead
of treating it at home. Your mind deserves the same
level of care as your body.

Stop expecting a timeline. — People will say, "It's
been a year." "You should be over it by now." "Time
heals all wounds." Ignore them. Your mind heals on its
own schedule, and no one else gets to set the clock.
The man who pressures himself to heal faster often
delays the healing. Give yourself the same patience you
would give a friend.

Rebuild the small routines first. — After trauma, the
big picture is too much. Start with the small things.
Make the bed. Eat a real meal. Go for a walk. Show up
at the same time every morning. These routines are not
trivial. They are the scaffolding that holds you upright
while the interior is being rebuilt. Structure is the

antidote to chaos — and after trauma, the mind craves structure more than answers.

Guard what you consume. — After trauma, the mind is porous. It absorbs content, noise, and energy in ways it didn't before. Be selective. Limit the news. Limit the content that triggers. Limit the conversations that drain. Surround your mind with things that rebuild — scripture, nature, silence, the voices of people who love you. What you consume after a wound either poisons it or heals it.

Move your body even when your mind doesn't want to. — The body stores trauma. The shoulders carry it. The stomach holds it. The chest constricts around it. Movement — walking, running, stretching, lifting — begins the process of releasing what the body has locked down. You will not feel like moving. Move anyway. The body often heals ahead of the mind and leads it out of the dark.

Write the story — all of it. — Not for publication. For processing. Write what happened. Write what you felt. Write what you lost. Write what you're afraid of now. Putting the story on paper takes it out of the loop in your head and gives it a container. A story written down is a story that can be examined, processed, and eventually closed. A story that stays in the head plays on repeat forever.

Let people love you through it. — Your instinct will be to isolate. To pull away from your wife, your friends, your church. Don't. Let them show up. Let them sit with you. Let them bring the meal, make the call, hold the silence. You don't have to talk. You don't have to be good company. You just have to let them in. The man who isolates after trauma doubles the weight he's carrying.

Believe that reconstruction is possible. — Not as a platitude. As a conviction. Men have rebuilt after losing everything — after war, after death, after betrayal that shattered their world. They rebuilt because they believed that the next chapter was still available to them. Believe it. Not because the evidence is clear — but because faith has never required clear evidence. Believe it, and then take the first step. That's how every reconstruction begins.

List 7: Ten Ways to Stop Living in Fear of What Might Happen

Name the fear. — The shapeless dread that sits in your chest at 2 a.m. has power precisely because it's shapeless. Name it. "I'm afraid of losing my job." "I'm afraid my marriage won't make it." "I'm afraid something will happen to my children." The moment you name it, it shrinks — not because the threat is gone, but because a named enemy is smaller than an invisible one.

Ask what you would do if it actually happened. — Play it out. The worst-case scenario arrives. Then what? You lose the job — you find another one. The marriage struggles — you get counseling. The diagnosis comes — you fight it. Most men are not afraid of the event. They are afraid of the unknown on the other side of the event. When you plan for the worst, the worst loses its power. Because you've already survived it in your mind.

Stop consuming content designed to make you afraid. — The news cycle is built on fear. The algorithm feeds you the worst-case scenario because outrage and anxiety generate clicks. And every click deepens the groove of anxiety in your brain. Limit the intake. Know what's happening in the world without marinating in it. Information is useful. Saturation is toxic.

Count what you have, not what you might lose. — Fear fixates on the threat. Gratitude fixates on the gift. You have a wife who loves you. Children who need you. A body that still works. A God who has never once failed to provide. When you shift your focus from what might be taken to what has already been given, the fear doesn't disappear — but it loses its grip on the steering wheel.

Live in today's trouble, not tomorrow's. — "Therefore do not worry about tomorrow, for tomorrow will worry about itself. Each day has enough trouble of its own." That's not wishful thinking. It is a command from the mouth of Christ. Today has its own problems. Solve those. Tomorrow's problems will arrive with tomorrow's grace. But if you borrow tomorrow's trouble and pile it on today's, you will collapse under a weight you were never meant to carry.

Distinguish between preparation and worry. — Saving money is preparation. Lying awake imagining bankruptcy is worry. Teaching your children safety is preparation. Catastrophizing every scenario is worry.

Preparation is productive. Worry is destructive. And the line between them is action. If the fear leads to a plan, it's preparation. If it leads to a spiral, it's worry. One deserves your attention. The other deserves to be dismissed.

Move your body when the fear is loud. — Anxiety lives in the body as much as the mind. The tight chest. The racing heart. The restless legs. When the fear gets loud, move. Walk fast. Run. Lift something heavy. The physical discharge of anxiety is one of the most effective tools available — and it requires no prescription, no appointment, and no explanation.

Tell someone. — "I've been afraid of this." That sentence, spoken to a wife, a brother, or a counselor, halves the weight immediately. Fear grows in the dark. It shrinks in the light. The man who carries his fear alone will be crushed by it. The man who speaks it out loud will find that the speaking itself was half the cure.

Remember what God has already brought you through. — The season you thought would break you didn't. The loss you thought was the end wasn't. The crisis that consumed your every waking thought eventually passed. You survived. God was faithful then. He will be faithful now. And the man who can remember past deliverance has the strongest weapon against present fear — evidence.

Act in the face of the fear. — Do the thing you're afraid of. Make the call. Apply for the job. Have the conversation. Start the venture. Fear tells you to freeze. Courage is not the absence of fear. It is the decision to move anyway. And every time you act in the

face of fear, the fear gets smaller — not because the
threat has changed, but because you have.

List 8: Ten Ways to Silence the Voice That Tells You You're Not Enough

Recognize it as a voice — not as truth. — The "not
enough" message is not a fact. It is a broadcast — one
that's been playing on repeat since someone first
planted the seed. A parent. A coach. A failure that
wrote itself into your identity. The first step to silencing
it is to recognize that it is a voice, not a verdict. You
can challenge a voice. You cannot argue with
something you've accepted as reality.

Trace it to its origin. — Where did the voice come
from? Who said it first? Was it the father who left and
made you believe you weren't worth staying for? The
teacher who said you'd never amount to anything? The
ex who told you you'd never change? The voice has an
origin. And when you identify the origin, you can
separate the message from the messenger — and you
can decide whether the messenger had the authority to
define you. They didn't.

Replace the lie with specific truth. — "You're not
enough" is a blanket statement. Counter it with
specifics. "I showed up for my family today. I kept my
word. I did the hard thing. I am growing." The lie is
vague. The truth must be precise. And the more precise
the truth, the less room the lie has to operate.

Stop measuring yourself against a moving target.
— Enough for whom? Enough by whose standard? The

internet's? Your father's? The culture's? The target is always moving — and a man who chases a moving target never arrives. Define your own standard. Root it in scripture, in character, in the values you've chosen. Then measure yourself against that — not against the ever-shifting scoreboard the world keeps changing.

Rehearse what God says about you. — You are fearfully and wonderfully made. You are chosen. You are loved. You are enough — not because of what you've done, but because of whose you are. These are not affirmations from a self-help book. They are declarations from the mouth of God. And the voice of God outranks the voice in your head every single time.

Do the thing the voice says you can't. — The voice says you're not smart enough to lead. Lead anyway. The voice says you're not strong enough to endure. Endure anyway. The voice says you'll fail. Try anyway. Every time you act in defiance of the voice, you weaken its authority. And over time, the voice doesn't stop — but it gets quieter. Because the evidence against it keeps growing.

Surround yourself with people who speak truth over you. — You need men in your life who say, "You're doing better than you think." Who say, "I see the growth." Who say, "You're a good father. You're a good man." Not flattery. Truth. The voice of a trusted brother is one of the most effective weapons against the internal liar. Let those voices in. Let them speak louder than the one in your head.

Stop comparing your interior to someone else's exterior. — You know your doubts, your fears, your failures, your darkest thoughts. You know none of that about the man you're comparing yourself to. You're comparing your raw footage to his final cut — and the comparison will always make you feel inadequate. It's a rigged game. Stop playing.

Accept that "enough" is not a destination. — You will never arrive at a place where the voice stops entirely. But you can reach a place where it no longer drives. Where you hear it, acknowledge it, and walk past it. That's not perfection. It's maturity. The man who waits to feel "enough" before he acts will wait forever. The man who acts despite feeling "not enough" is the man who builds a life worth admiring.

Let your scars be your credentials. — The voice says your failures disqualify you. The truth says they qualify you. The man who has failed and gotten back up has something the untested man does not — proof. Proof that he can survive what breaks other men. Proof that his character held when the pressure didn't relent. Your scars are not evidence that you're not enough. They are evidence that you're still here. And still here is more than enough.

List 9: Ten Ways to Be Patient When Everything in You Wants to Quit

Remember that quitting is permanent and feelings are temporary. — The frustration you feel right now will not be the frustration you feel in a month. But the consequences of quitting will still be there. Feelings are weather. They change. Decisions are architecture. They remain. Don't build your life around today's storm. The man who can distinguish between a passing feeling and a permanent decision is the man who avoids the regrets that haunt men who quit too soon.

Go back to the original reason. — Why did you start? What was the conviction, the vision, the purpose? Write it down again. Read it out loud. The man who forgets his why will always be defeated by his how. And the how is always harder than anyone expected. But the why — if it's real — is enough to carry you through the how.

Shrink the horizon. — Stop looking at the whole road. You don't need to see the finish line. You need to see the next mile. The next day. The next hour. Patience is not the ability to see forever. It is the ability to take the next step without demanding to know where the road ends. The man who can shrink the horizon can endure almost anything — because almost anything is survivable for one more day.

Talk to someone who's further down the same path. — The man who has been married for thirty years. The man who built the business over a decade. The man who has walked with God through seasons of silence. Ask him: "Did you want to quit?" He'll say yes. Ask him: "Why didn't you?" His answer is your fuel. And his presence is proof that the road you're walking has been walked before.

Celebrate what has already been built. — You're so focused on what's not working that you've forgotten what is. Look at what you've done. The marriage that's still standing. The children who are growing. The faith that's still breathing. The work that's still producing. You are not failing as badly as you think. The man who can celebrate the progress finds the energy to endure the process.

Accept the season. — Not every season is harvest. Some seasons are planting. Some are waiting. Some are winter — cold, dark, and seemingly barren. But winter is not the end of the story. It is the part of the story where roots grow deeper because nothing else can grow. Accept the season. Don't try to harvest in planting season. Don't demand fruit in winter. Trust the cycle. The man who understands seasons is the man who survives them.

Stop comparing your timeline to someone else's. — The man who built it in two years started with advantages you didn't have. The man who seems ahead of you may have left behind things you refused to sacrifice. Your timeline is yours. It is not late. It is not behind. It is exactly where a man who refused to cut corners and kept walking ends up. Patience is the refusal to adopt someone else's clock.

Fast from the content that makes you want to quit. — The feeds that show you the success you haven't reached. The comparisons that make your effort feel small. The highlight reels that obscure the truth of how long real success takes. Remove the inputs that feed impatience. Replace them with inputs that feed endurance — books, mentors, scripture, silence.

Do one thing today that moves you forward, no matter how small. — Write one page. Make one call.

Complete one task. Movement — even tiny movement — is the antidote to the paralysis that comes before quitting. The man who does one thing today has done infinitely more than the man who quit yesterday. Keep moving. The speed doesn't matter. The direction does.

Pray for endurance, not escape. — The natural prayer in pain is, "Get me out of this." The mature prayer is, "Give me the strength to walk through it." Escape removes the lesson. Endurance completes it. And the man who has endured is the man who emerges with something the man who escaped will never have — the unshakeable confidence that he can survive whatever comes next. Because he already has.

List 10: Ten Ways to Find Peace in the Middle of the Storm

Stop demanding that the storm end before you find peace. — Peace is not the absence of the storm. It is the presence of something greater inside you than the chaos around you. The man who waits for calm seas before he finds peace will spend his entire life in turmoil — because the seas never stay calm for long.

Control what you can and release what you can't. — You can control your response. You cannot control the outcome. You can control your effort. You cannot control the result. You can control your attitude. You cannot control other people's behavior. The man who draws a clear line between what's his and what's God's finds a peace that the man who tries to manage everything never will.

Pray before you panic. — The instinct is to react — to call someone, to solve something, to move immediately. Resist. Before the first phone call, before the first plan, before the first word — pray. "God, I can't see the way through this. Show me." That prayer, spoken in the first sixty seconds of the storm, repositions everything that follows.

Simplify your life during the crisis. — Drop the unnecessary. Cancel the optional. Reduce the noise. When the storm hits, your margin disappears — so create some. Fewer commitments. Fewer distractions. Fewer obligations that are not essential. Peace in the storm requires space, and space requires saying no to everything that is not absolutely necessary.

Stay in the present moment. — The storm tempts you to live in the future — to catastrophize, to predict, to imagine the worst. Come back to now. Right now, in this moment, you are alive. You are breathing. You have not been destroyed. The present is the only place peace can live. The future is the only place anxiety can grow. Choose where to stand.

Sit with someone who has known peace in their own storm. — Not the man who has all the answers. The man who has survived without them. The man who walked through the fire and came out with a quiet steadiness that no circumstance can explain. Sit with that man. Let his peace be contagious. You do not need advice. You need proximity to a man whose anchor held.

Read the psalms. — They were written by men in storms — men running from kings, mourning dead children, hiding in caves, watching their kingdoms crumble. And yet they end, almost always, with a declaration of trust. "Even though I walk through the valley of the shadow of death, I will fear no evil, for you are with me." Those words were not written by comfortable men. They were written by men who found peace in the exact place you're standing.

Limit how much you talk about the storm. — Processing is necessary. Rehearsing is destructive. There is a point at which talking about the crisis stops being therapeutic and starts being recursive — a loop that keeps the anxiety alive by giving it fresh oxygen every time you narrate it. Process with one or two people. Then stop. Let the silence do its work.

Serve someone else. — In the middle of your own storm, serve a man in his. Bring the meal. Make the call. Sit with the grieving. Something shifts when you step outside your own pain long enough to attend to someone else's. Your storm doesn't shrink — but your perspective expands. And expanded perspective is the closest thing to peace a man can find in the middle of the wind.

Anchor yourself in the unchanging. — Everything around you is shifting. The finances. The diagnosis. The relationship. The plan. But there is something that does not shift — the character of God, the love of God, the promises of God. Anchor there. Not because you understand what He's doing. But because you trust who He is. That anchor — driven into the bedrock of something eternal — is the only thing that holds when everything else gives way.

MENTAL TOUGHNESS: QUOTES

"I have told you these things, so that in me you may have peace. In this world you will have trouble. But take heart! I have overcome the world." —John 16:33

"We are hard pressed on every side, but not crushed; perplexed, but not in despair; persecuted, but not abandoned; struck down, but not destroyed." —2 Corinthians 4:8-9

"If I'm going to fall, I don't want to fall back on anything except my faith. I want to fall forward." —Denzel Washington, UPenn Commencement, 2011

"You can't always control circumstances. However, you can always control your attitude, approach, and response." —Tony Dungy, *Quiet Strength*

"What God knows about us is more important than what others think." —Tim Tebow, *Shaken*

"You are imperfect. You always will be. But there is a powerful force that designed you that way, and if you're willing to accept that, you will have grace." —Chris Pratt, 2018 MTV Movie & TV Awards

"Consider it pure joy, my brothers and sisters, whenever you face trials of many kinds, because you know that the testing of your faith produces perseverance." —James 1:2-3

"Be strong and courageous. Do not be afraid or terrified because of them, for the Lord your God goes with you; he will never leave you nor forsake you." —Deuteronomy 31:6

"I'm not perfect. I'm never going to be. And that's the great thing about living the Christian life and trying to live by faith, is you're trying to get better every day." — Tim Tebow

"You gain strength, courage, and confidence by every experience in which you really stop to look fear in the face." —Eleanor Roosevelt

MENTAL TOUGHNESS: PUTTING IT INTO PRACTICE

Name one fear you've been carrying and tell someone this week. — Not publicly. Privately. One man. One conversation. "I've been afraid of this." The weight halves the moment it's spoken.

The next time you feel anger rising, pause for ten full seconds before responding. — Count them. Breathe through them. Let the impulse pass. Then respond — not react. That ten-second discipline will change every relationship in your life.

Write down the three things consuming your mental energy right now. — Next to each one, write: "Can I control this?" If yes, make a plan. If no, write "I release this." The act of writing the release gives the mind permission to let go.

Turn off all news and social media for one full day this week. — One day. No scrolling. No checking. No consuming. Notice how your mind feels by evening. The difference will tell you how much noise you've been carrying without realizing it.

Identify the internal voice that says "you're not enough" — and write a response to it. — In your own handwriting. "You say I'm not enough. Here's what's actually true: I showed up today. I kept my word. I'm still standing." Keep the page. Read it when the voice gets loud.

When the urge to quit hits this week, shrink the horizon. — Don't look at the whole mountain. Ask: "Can I make it through today?" If yes, do that. Tomorrow you'll ask again. Patience is built one day at a time, not one year at a time.

Spend twenty minutes this week sitting in complete silence. — No music. No screen. No book. Just you and your thoughts. Let them come. Let them pass. Practice being present with yourself without reaching for a distraction. This is the training ground for every storm you'll ever face.

Write down one thing you survived that you once thought would destroy you. — Hold it as evidence. You made it through that. You will make it through this. Past endurance is the most reliable predictor of future endurance.

Exercise at least three times this week — specifically to regulate your emotions. — Not for aesthetics. For mental health. Walk when you're anxious. Run when you're angry. Lift when you feel powerless. The body and the mind are not separate systems. Train one to heal the other.

Before bed each night this week, read one psalm. — Start with Psalm 23. Then 27. Then 46. Then 91. Then 121. These were written by men in storms — and they found peace anyway. Let their words become yours.

CATEGORY 9

LEGACY & PURPOSE

List 1: Ten Ways to Live for Something Bigger Than Yourself

Ask the question most men avoid. — "What am I here for?" Not what you do for a living. Not what role you play in your family. What is the reason you exist? Most men never ask because the answer demands change — and change is expensive. But a man who never asks the question lives an unexamined life. And an unexamined life, no matter how successful, is a life that drifts.

Anchor your purpose in something that doesn't expire. — Titles expire. Paychecks expire. Physical strength expires. Fame expires. If your purpose is tied to anything temporary, your purpose has a shelf life. Anchor it in the eternal — in faith, in service, in the formation of people who will outlive you. A man whose purpose is rooted in the permanent is a man who never loses his reason to get up in the morning.

Serve without recognition. — The man who serves to be seen has already received his reward — and it is

234

small. The man who serves in the dark, who gives anonymously, who works behind the scenes with no expectation of credit — that man is building something the first man will never understand. Purpose is not a performance. It is a posture. And the posture is bent toward others, not toward applause.

Invest in people who will never repay you. — The child in the mentoring program. The neighbor who needs help but can't return the favor. The stranger whose name you'll never know. Purpose is not transactional. It is not a return on investment. It is the deliberate decision to pour yourself into something that benefits someone other than you — with no expectation of reciprocity.

Live with the awareness that your days are numbered. — Not as morbid fixation. As urgent clarity. You have a limited number of mornings. A limited number of dinners with your children. A limited number of Sundays. When you live with that awareness, the trivial falls away and the essential rises to the surface. The man who knows his time is finite spends it differently than the man who lives as though he has forever.

Build something that will still be standing when you're gone. — A family that knows God. A business with integrity baked into the walls. A community that was better because you lived in it. A faith that your grandchildren will carry. The man who builds only for himself builds a sandcastle. The man who builds for others builds a cathedral.

Say no to the things that don't align with your purpose. — Every invitation is not a calling. Every opportunity is not a mission. The man who says yes to everything dilutes his impact across a hundred surfaces — an inch deep on all of them. The man who says no to what doesn't matter can say a thundering yes to what does.

Give your best hours to the most important things. — Most men give their best energy to their employer and their leftover energy to their family, their faith, and their community. Reverse it. Give the first and best to the things that matter most. The inbox will survive your neglect. Your children will not.

Leave every room, every job, every season better than you found it. — That is purpose in its simplest form. Not the grand gesture. The daily deposit. Did the meeting improve because you were in it? Did the neighborhood benefit from your presence? Did the conversation leave the other person stronger? Purpose is not one moment. It is a thousand small ones — each one bent toward the good of someone else.

Let God define your assignment. — You don't get to choose your purpose. You get to discover it. And the discovery comes not from a career assessment but from a conversation with the One who made you. "God, what did You put me here to do?" That question, asked with genuine surrender, is the beginning of a life that matters. And the man who asks it — and obeys the answer — will never wonder again whether his life counted.

List 2: Ten Ways to Build Something That Will Outlast You

Pour into your children's character, not just their comfort. — The house will depreciate. The car will rust. The inheritance will be spent. But the character you build into your children — the honesty, the discipline, the faith, the integrity — will compound across generations. A man who raises children of character has built something that will outlive every material thing he owns.

Write it down. — Your story. Your lessons. Your failures. Your convictions. The things you wish someone had told you. Put them on paper. Not for publication — for preservation. A man who writes nothing leaves his children guessing. A man who writes the truth leaves them a map. And maps are passed from hand to hand long after the cartographer is gone.

Build a marriage that your grandchildren will want to imitate. — They are watching — not just your children, but their children's children. The way you love your wife today is writing the script for marriages that haven't started yet. A man who loves his wife well for fifty years has built the most visible and enduring structure available to any human being.

Plant trees you'll never sit under. — Give to the fund that won't pay off until your grandchildren are grown. Build the system at work that your successor will benefit from. Invest in the young man who won't reach his potential until long after you've gone. The man who plants trees he'll never sit under is the man who has transcended his own timeline.

Create traditions that carry your values. — The family dinner every Sunday. The prayer before every meal. The annual trip. The letter on every birthday. These are not rituals. They are value-delivery systems. They carry what you believe into the lives of people who may not remember your words but will never forget your rhythms.

Mentor younger men deliberately. — One generation teaches the next. That's how civilization works. The man who pours his experience, his failures, his wisdom into a younger man has multiplied himself in the most meaningful way possible. You won't live forever. But the men you shaped will carry pieces of you into rooms you'll never enter.

Serve your community visibly and consistently. — Not for the recognition. For the record. When your children see you serve — at the church, at the shelter, at the school — they learn that a man's life is measured not by what he accumulated but by what he gave. That lesson, modeled consistently, becomes the operating system for the next generation.

Build your reputation on integrity, not on success. — Success is circumstantial. Integrity is chosen. The man who is known for his honesty, his reliability, and his character has built a reputation that survives career changes, market crashes, and generational shifts. Success fades from memory. Character becomes legend.

Leave your faith as the cornerstone. — Of everything you build — your family, your business, your community — let faith be the foundation. Not a decorative addition. The load-bearing wall. A man who leaves behind a thriving faith in his family has built the one thing that fire, flood, and time cannot destroy.

Live so that your funeral is a testimony. — Not a performance. A testimony. When the people who knew you stand up to speak, what will they say? That you made money? That you were busy? Or that you loved deeply, served tirelessly, and pointed every person in your life toward something greater than yourself? The eulogy is the final review. Live now the way you want to be remembered then.

List 3: Ten Ways to Find Your Purpose When the World Says You Don't Have One

Reject the lie that purpose is a luxury. — The world will tell you that purpose is for dreamers, for the privileged, for people with time to think about such things. It's a lie. Purpose is the birthright of every man who draws breath. You were not made to exist. You were made to matter. And the search for that meaning is not a distraction from life — it is the point of it.

Look at what makes you angry. — Righteous anger is a compass. What injustice makes your blood boil? What brokenness makes you want to act? The thing that angers you most may be the thing you were built to fight. Not every man is called to the same battle. But every man is called to one. Your anger might be pointing you to yours.

Look at what breaks your heart. — The orphan. The addict. The fatherless boy. The forgotten elderly. The community falling apart. What breaks your heart is often the doorway to your calling. Purpose lives at the intersection of your gifting and the world's need — and the world's need is most visible to the man whose heart is soft enough to see it.

Look at what you do when no one is watching. — The thing you do for free. The thing you'd do even if it never paid. The skill you practice without being asked. These are not hobbies. They are clues. Purpose is not always dramatic. Sometimes it's the quiet thing you've been doing all along that no one — including you — recognized as your calling.

Ask the people closest to you what they see in you. — Your wife. Your friend. Your mentor. Ask them: "What do you think I was made to do?" Sometimes the people who love you can see your purpose more clearly than you can — because they're standing far enough away to see the whole picture.

Stop waiting for a burning bush. — Most men never find their purpose because they're waiting for a dramatic revelation. A voice from heaven. A sign in the sky. It rarely works that way. More often, purpose reveals itself in the ordinary — in the consistent pull toward a specific kind of work, a specific kind of person, a specific kind of problem. Pay attention to the pull. It's been there longer than you think.

Try things. — You will not discover your purpose from a couch. Get out. Volunteer. Serve. Build. Fail. Start over. Purpose is discovered in motion, not in meditation. The man who tries ten things and fails at eight has learned more about himself than the man who thought about trying and never moved.

Read the stories of men who found their purpose late. — Moses was eighty. Abraham was seventy-five. Some of the most purposeful lives in history didn't start until the second half. If you feel behind, you're not. You're on schedule — a schedule that doesn't look like the world's timeline because it was written by a God who doesn't rush.

Align your gifts with the needs around you. — You have skills. You have experience. You have a temperament uniquely designed for a specific kind of impact. The question is: where does your gifting meet the world's need? That intersection is your assignment. And when you find it, the work won't feel like work. It will feel like the thing you were always supposed to be doing.

Surrender the search to God. — "God, I don't know what I'm here for. But I'm willing to do whatever You show me." That prayer — spoken with genuine surrender — is the most powerful purpose-finding tool in existence. Because purpose is not something you manufacture. It is something you receive. And the man who asks with open hands will receive an answer that closed fists could never hold.

List 4: Ten Ways to Leave a Legacy That Has Nothing to Do with Money

Be remembered for how you made people feel. — No one will remember your net worth. They will remember whether you made them feel seen, valued, and known. The man who leaves behind a trail of people who felt loved in his presence has left the richest legacy available — one that no market crash can diminish and no inflation can erode.

Tell the truth — always. — A legacy of honesty is a legacy of safety. The man who was known for telling the truth, even when it cost him, leaves behind a name that his children can carry without shame. Honest men raise honest families. And honest families change the trajectory of communities that have been drowning in deception.

Keep your promises. — Every promise kept is a brick in the wall of your legacy. Every promise broken is a crack. The man who was known for his word — who said what he meant and did what he said — leaves behind a reputation that his grandchildren will inherit like a family treasure.

Show up. — At the game. At the recital. At the hospital. At the funeral. At the 2 a.m. phone call. The man who showed up — consistently, faithfully, without being asked — will be remembered not for what he did, but for the fact that he was always there. Presence is the most undervalued legacy a man can leave.

Forgive generously. — The man who forgave — his father, his friend, his enemy — leaves behind a legacy of freedom. His children will learn that grudges are prisons and that forgiveness is the key. And they will pass that freedom to their children, and their children's children. A forgiving man doesn't just free himself. He frees a lineage.

Love your wife in a way your children never forget.
— They will forget the house. They will forget the
vacations. They will not forget how their father looked
at their mother. The way you loved your wife is the
most visible, most imitable, most permanent legacy you
will ever build. Love her well, and your legacy will echo
in marriages you never witness.

Pray for people by name. — The man who prayed —
not publicly, not performatively, but privately,
consistently, by name — leaves behind a legacy that
operates in the invisible realm. You may never know
the full impact of a prayer offered on behalf of another
person. But the impact is real. And it outlasts
everything you can build with your hands.

Be kind to strangers. — The tip that changed the
waitress's night. The word of encouragement to the kid
who was struggling. The time you stopped to help the
man on the side of the road. These moments —
invisible, unrecorded, unrewarded — are the fabric of a
legacy that doesn't make the news but changes the
world anyway.

Leave behind letters. — To your wife. To each of your
children. To your closest friend. Write what you want
them to know after you're gone. Not a will — a witness.
A letter that says, "Here is what you meant to me. Here
is what I hope for you. Here is what I believe." A letter
from a dead man is one of the most powerful
documents a family can possess.

**Live with integrity so relentless that your name
becomes a standard.** — "He was a man of his word."
"He was the real deal." "He lived what he preached."

When your name becomes a reference point — the standard by which other men measure themselves — you have left a legacy that no obituary can capture and no gravestone can contain.

List 5: Ten Ways to Write a Story with Your Life That's Worth Telling

Decide what story you want to tell — and start living it. — You are both the author and the character. The choices you make today are the chapters your children will read tomorrow. If the story you're writing is about comfort, safety, and the avoidance of risk — it's not a story anyone will want to hear. Write a story about a man who dared, who sacrificed, who loved, who built, who fell and got back up.

Stop editing your past and start writing your future. — You cannot change the chapters that have already been written. The failure. The divorce. The addiction. The wasted years. Those pages are done. But the pen is still in your hand, and the remaining pages are blank. The question is not what you've written. It is what you will write next.

Include the failures. — The best stories are not the ones where the hero never stumbles. They are the ones where the hero falls — hard — and rises anyway. Your failures are not disqualifications. They are plot points. And the man who is honest about his failures gives permission to every man reading his story to be honest about theirs.

Write with courage, not with comfort. — The story of a man who played it safe has never inspired anyone. Take the risk. Start the business. Have the conversation. Move to the city. Leave the thing that's killing you. The chapters worth reading are the ones that cost the author something. Write those.

Make other people the heroes of your story. — The best-written life is not the one where the man stands in the center of every frame. It is the one where the man lifts others into the frame with him. Your wife. Your children. Your friends. Your mentees. The story of a man who made other people great is a better story than the story of a man who made himself famous.

Let the hard chapters shape you. — The diagnosis. The layoff. The broken relationship. The season of doubt. These are not interruptions to your story. They are the chapters that give the rest of the story its weight. A man who has only known ease has a thin story. A man who has walked through fire has one worth telling.

Write chapters that surprise people. — The comeback. The forgiveness no one expected. The career change at fifty. The apology that came twenty years late. The risk that everyone said was crazy. Surprise is the sign of a man who is still alive — still growing, still changing, still refusing to let the world write his ending.

Don't let someone else hold the pen. — Your boss doesn't write your story. Your father didn't finish it. Your past doesn't own it. The culture doesn't dictate it. You — under the authorship of God — hold the pen.

And the man who reclaims authorship of his own life is the man who writes something worth reading.

Write it for an audience of One. — Not the internet. Not the crowd. Not the colleagues. Write it for God. Live your life as though the only review that matters is the one you'll receive at the end — from the One who saw every private act, every hidden sacrifice, every quiet prayer. That audience is enough. It has always been enough.

Finish strong. — The opening of the story matters. But the ending matters more. A man who lived well in his twenties but coasted through his sixties has written a story with a weak ending. A man who stumbled through his thirties but finished his seventies with integrity, faith, and love has written a masterpiece. The final chapters define the whole. Write them with everything you have.

List 6: Ten Ways to Invest in the Next Generation When No One Invested in You

Decide that the chain breaks with you. — No one poured into you. No one showed you the way. No one believed in you when it mattered. That's real. That's painful. And it ends now. You are the man who stands in the gap — the one who says, "No boy behind me will walk this road alone because I walked it alone and I know what it costs." That decision is the most important one you'll ever make.

Start with one young man. — You don't need a program. You don't need a title. You need one kid, one conversation, one hour a week. Buy him lunch. Ask him what he's dealing with. Listen without lecturing. Show up the next week. And the next. Consistency is the language of investment — and a young man who has never had a consistent man in his life will recognize it immediately.

Share what you wished someone had told you. — "Here's what I learned the hard way." "Here's what I wish my father had said." "Here's what no one told me about marriage, money, anger, faith." Your scars are your curriculum. The lessons you paid for in pain are the ones that carry the most weight when spoken into a younger man's life.

Don't try to be perfect — be present. — The young man in front of you doesn't need a flawless mentor. He needs a real one. One who admits his failures, laughs at his own mistakes, and shows up even when he doesn't have the right words. Presence, not perfection, is what builds trust. And trust is the foundation of every investment that actually takes root.

Believe in him before he believes in himself. — Speak to the man he's becoming, not the boy he is today. "You're going to be a great father." "You have what it takes to lead." "I see something in you that you haven't seen yet." Those words, spoken by a man he respects, become the architecture of his future identity. Most young men are only one sentence away from believing they can become something.

Open doors he doesn't know exist. — Bring him to the job site. Introduce him to the mentor. Invite him to the meeting. Give him the book that changed your life.

Exposure is one of the most powerful gifts you can give a young man who grew up without access. He can't aspire to what he's never seen. Show him what's possible.

Hold him accountable without giving up on him. — He will let you down. He will make the same mistake twice. He will test you the way every fatherless boy tests every man who gets close — pushing to see if you'll leave like the others did. Don't leave. Hold the line. Correct him. Then show up the next week. The man who stays through the testing is the man who earns the trust that transforms.

Teach him the invisible skills. — How to shake a hand. How to look someone in the eye. How to manage money. How to disagree without disrespecting. How to treat a woman. How to handle failure. How to sit in a job interview. How to apologize. These are the skills that separate men who thrive from men who survive — and they are only transmitted through relationship.

Pray for him. — By name. Daily. For his protection, his growth, his future wife, his future children, his purpose. Prayer is the ultimate investment — the one that operates beyond your ability and reach. And the man who prays for a young man's future is shaping that future in ways no human effort can replicate.

Let him see the fruit of your investment — and then send him to do the same. — The goal is not to create a follower. It is to create another investor. When the young man you poured into begins to pour into someone else, the chain is not just repaired. It is multiplied. And that multiplication — that cascade of

investment from one generation to the next — is the
most enduring legacy a man can build.

List 7: Ten Ways to Live with Urgency Without Living with Anxiety

Accept that time is finite — and let that fuel you, not frighten you. — You don't have forever. That's not a threat. It's a gift. The awareness of your own mortality is the most powerful motivator available — if you let it drive you toward purpose rather than panic. The man who accepts his limits doesn't freeze. He focuses.

Do the important thing today, not tomorrow. — Tomorrow is not promised. And even if it comes, it will arrive with its own demands. The conversation you need to have. The letter you need to write. The relationship you need to repair. Do it today. Urgency is not about speed. It is about refusing to postpone the things that matter.

Separate urgency from hurry. — Urgency is clarity about what matters and the discipline to act on it. Hurry is frenzy. Urgency writes the letter today because life is short. Hurry sends the email while driving because everything feels like an emergency. The first is wisdom. The second is self-destruction. Know the difference.

Eliminate the time-wasters. — The scroll that consumes an hour. The content that adds nothing. The obligation that serves no one. The commitment that drains you and produces nothing of value. A man who lives with urgency audits his time the way a wise man audits his budget — and he cuts what doesn't serve the mission.

Build margin for the unexpected. — Urgency without margin produces anxiety. Leave space in your day for the conversation you didn't plan. The crisis that arrives uninvited. The moment with your child that can't be scheduled. A man who fills every minute has no room for the sacred interruptions that often matter more than the agenda.

Focus on three things at a time. — Not ten. Not twenty. Three. What are the three most important things in this season? Maybe it's your marriage, your health, and your faith. Maybe it's your business, your son, and your sobriety. Name them. Protect them. Let everything else wait. Urgency is not doing everything. It is doing the right things with everything you have.

Stop living as if you'll get to it later. — Later is the graveyard of intention. Later is where the apology dies. Later is where the dream decays. Later is where the letter you should have written gathers dust until the funeral forces you to wish you'd written it sooner. Stop saying later. Start saying now.

End each day with an honest assessment. — Did I spend today on what mattered? Did I give my presence to the people who deserve it? Did I move the needle on the thing God put in front of me? This daily review is not guilt. It is calibration. And a man who calibrates daily lives a life that doesn't need a midlife crisis to correct it.

Rest as part of the urgency, not against it. — The urgent man rests because rest sharpens him. Rest is not wasted time. It is preparation for the next day's purpose. The man who burns out has not lived urgently. He has lived carelessly. True urgency includes the discipline to stop — because a broken man can do nothing urgent at all.

Hold it all loosely. — Live with urgency, but hold the outcomes with open hands. You cannot control results. You can control effort, intention, and faithfulness. The man who lives urgently and holds loosely has found the balance most men spend their entire lives searching for — the ability to care deeply and surrender fully at the same time.

List 8: Ten Ways to Measure Your Life by What You Gave, Not What You Got

Count the people, not the possessions. — At the end of your life, the inventory that matters is not what you owned but who you loved. How many men did you mentor? How many meals did you share? How many people are standing because you held them up? The man who counts relationships instead of assets dies rich — regardless of his bank balance.

Give your time before your money. — Money is replaceable. Time is not. The hour you spent with your son. The afternoon you gave to the struggling neighbor. The evening you sat with a grieving friend instead of watching the game. These are the most expensive gifts a man can give — and the most valuable.

Celebrate the success of others without needing your own. — A man who can genuinely rejoice in another man's win — without jealousy, without comparison, without the need to match it — is a man who has untethered his worth from his outcomes. That freedom is rare. And it produces a generosity of spirit that draws people in and keeps them close.

Give anonymously. — The donation no one traces back to you. The bill you paid for the family behind you. The gift that arrived without a name attached. Anonymous giving is the purest test of your generosity — because it removes the only selfish incentive left: the applause. The man who gives in secret knows who he's really giving to.

Mentor without a scoreboard. — The temptation in mentoring is to track the outcome — did he get the promotion? Did he stay clean? Did he change? But the man who mentors without a scoreboard gives freely, knowing that the seed he planted may not sprout in his lifetime. Plant anyway. Water anyway. The harvest belongs to God.

Ask your family what they need — not what you want to give. — Provision is not dictated by the provider. It is shaped by the receiver. Your wife may not need the bigger house. She may need your undivided attention on a Tuesday night. Your son may not need the expensive camp. He may need you to sit in the bleachers. Give what they need. Not what makes you feel generous.

Leave every room having added something. — Encouragement. Clarity. Calm. A kind word. A genuine compliment. A question that made someone think. The man who adds value to every room he enters has lived a life of giving without ever writing a check.

Sacrifice comfort for someone else's benefit. — Wake up early to drive your wife so she doesn't have to go alone. Skip the game to sit with the friend who's falling apart. Give up the weekend to help the neighbor move. These are not grand sacrifices. They are daily ones. And daily sacrifice, compounded over a lifetime, builds a legacy of selflessness that grand gestures cannot match.

Teach your children to give before they learn to earn. — Before they understand money, teach them generosity. Share the toy. Help the friend. Give the coat to the kid who doesn't have one. A child who learns to give before he learns to accumulate will become a man who measures his life by the right standard from the start.

On your last day, let the ledger read "gave" more than "got." — That is the only math that matters. Not what you earned. What you gave. Not what you built. What you built into others. Not what you owned. What you released. The man whose giving outpaces his getting is the man whose life was worth the breath God put in his lungs.

List 9: Ten Ways to Make Every Year Count After Forty

Stop coasting. — Forty is not the beginning of the end. It is the beginning of the part that actually matters. You have experience now. Wisdom. Scar tissue. Perspective. The man who coasts after forty wastes the most productive and meaningful decades of his life. This is not the time to slow down. This is the time to aim.

Audit your relationships. — Who is sharpening you? Who is draining you? Who have you neglected? After forty, your time is too valuable and too short to spend on relationships that produce nothing. Deepen the ones that matter. Release the ones that don't. And repair the ones you broke when you were too young to know better.

Get your health in order. — The body you ignored in your thirties will present the bill in your fifties. Get the checkup. Fix the diet. Start the exercise. Sleep like it matters. The man who enters his fifties healthy has bought himself decades of capacity. The man who enters sick has shortened every runway he has.

Write the letter you've been putting off. — To your father. To your son. To the friend you lost touch with. To the mentor who changed your life. Write it now. Not because you're dying — because you're alive. And alive is the only window you have to say the things that matter.

Learn something new every year. — A skill. A language. A discipline. A subject you've never explored. The man who stops learning after forty is the man who stops growing. And the man who stops growing is the man who starts shrinking — mentally, spiritually, and relationally.

Invest in the next generation with the urgency of a man who knows his time is limited. — Mentor harder. Teach more. Give more freely. The men behind you need what you've learned, and you don't have forever to deliver it. Every year after forty is a year that counts double — because the lessons you pass on now will outlive you.

Simplify. — Less stuff. Fewer commitments. Smaller ambitions that carry bigger meaning. The second half of life is not about accumulation. It is about distillation — boiling everything down to the essential and pouring yourself into that. The man who simplifies after forty finds a freedom the man who adds more will never know.

Forgive what you've been carrying. — The grudge from your twenties. The resentment from your thirties. The wound you've been nursing for decades. Let it go. Not because it didn't matter. Because carrying it is costing you years you can't afford to lose. Forgiveness after forty is not generosity. It is survival.

Date your wife like you're running out of time. — Because you are. The children will leave. The house will empty. And the two of you will be sitting across from each other with either a rich history of continued pursuit — or the hollow realization that you stopped trying somewhere around year fifteen. Pursue her now. Every year. Like the gift she is.

Live every remaining year like it's a letter to your grandchildren. — What will they know about you? What will they learn from the way you spent your fifties, your sixties, your seventies? Every year is a page. Every decision is a sentence. Write it with the awareness that someone who hasn't been born yet will one day read it — and decide what kind of man they want to become based on what you wrote.

List 10: Ten Ways to Die with Nothing Left Undone and Nothing Left Unsaid

Tell the people you love what they mean to you — today. — Don't wait for the diagnosis. Don't wait for the funeral. Don't wait for the regret that comes from standing over a grave and wishing you'd said the words when the person could hear them. Say it now. To your wife. To your children. To your brother. To your friend. "You matter to me. Here's why."

Forgive everyone. — Not because they deserve it. Because you do. The man who dies carrying unforgiveness dies in a prison he built himself. Release it. All of it. The father who left. The friend who betrayed. The boss who stole your credit. Let it go — not for them, but for the peace that will fill the space the bitterness occupied.

Apologize to the people you've hurt. — Don't assume they've forgotten. They haven't. The man you belittled at work. The friend you ghosted. The wife you neglected for years. The child you were too harsh with. Find them. Say the words: "I was wrong. I'm sorry." That sentence, delivered sincerely, can heal a wound that's been open for decades.

Get your affairs in order. — The will. The accounts. The insurance. The passwords. The instructions. The preferences. A man who dies without his affairs in order has left his family a burden disguised as a mystery. Get it done. Not because you're dying soon — because you love them too much to leave them scrambling when you do.

Finish the project. — The book you've been writing. The business you've been planning. The skill you've been learning. The relationship you've been building. Finish it. The unfinished project is the heaviest ghost — the one that whispers, "You could have, but you didn't." Don't leave that ghost for your family to live with.

Have the conversation you've been avoiding. — With your son about your past. With your wife about your fears. With your father about what he did — or didn't do. The conversation you avoid in life becomes the conversation your family has about you after death. Have it now, while there's still time for it to change something.

Make peace with God. — Whatever that means for you — the rededication, the first commitment, the return after years away — do it. The man who dies at peace with his Creator dies at peace with everything. And the man who doesn't carries a weight into eternity that no earthly resolution could ever match.

Leave instructions for how you want to be remembered. — Not the logistics of the funeral. The spirit of it. "I want them to laugh. I want them to know I loved God. I want the focus to be on Him, not on me." Give your family the gift of knowing how to honor you — so they don't have to guess while they're grieving.

Spend your final years giving everything away. — Your knowledge. Your time. Your resources. Your stories. Your faith. The man who arrives at death with empty hands and a full legacy has lived the only way a man should live. Grip nothing. Give everything. And when the end comes, you will not be afraid — because there's nothing left to hold onto and nothing left to regret.

Live today as if it were the last page. — Not with recklessness. With intention. With the sharp awareness that the man you are today is the man they'll remember. Make the call. Write the letter. Hold her hand. Pray the prayer. Tell the truth. Do the work. And when the final page turns, let the story close with a man who left nothing in the margins — no unlived love, no unspoken truth, no ungiven gift. That's how a man dies well. He lives well first.

LEGACY & PURPOSE: QUOTES

"For what shall it profit a man, if he shall gain the whole world, and lose his own soul?" —Mark 8:36

"The two most important days in your life are the day you are born and the day you find out why." — Attributed to Mark Twain

"Success comes in a lot of ways, but it doesn't come with money and it doesn't come with fame. It comes from having a meaning in your life." —Tim Tebow

"What will people remember us for? Are other people's lives better because we lived? Did we make a difference?" —Tony Dungy, *Quiet Strength*

"A good man leaves an inheritance to his children's children." —Proverbs 13:22

"You've got to get out there and give it everything you got. Whether it's your time, your talent, your prayers, or your treasures." —Denzel Washington, Dillard University Commencement, 2015

"I have fought the good fight, I have finished the race, I have kept the faith." —2 Timothy 4:7

"I've been put in this position for a reason, it's not to forget about where I came from. I have to utilize these talents and gifts that have been given to me to help others." —Mark Wahlberg

"He has shown you, O mortal, what is good. And what does the Lord require of you? To act justly and to love mercy and to walk humbly with your God." —Micah 6:8

"It's about the journey — mine and yours — and the lives we can touch, the legacy we can leave, and the world we can change for the better." —Tony Dungy

---

LEGACY & PURPOSE: PUTTING IT INTO PRACTICE

Write a one-page purpose statement this week. — In your own words, answer: "Why am I here? What am I building? Who am I serving? What will I leave behind?" Read it every morning for a month. Revise it as clarity grows.

Write a letter to each of your children this week.
— Not a text. A handwritten letter. Tell them what you
see in them. Tell them what you're proud of. Tell them
what you hope for their future. They will keep these
letters for the rest of their lives.

**Identify one young man and begin meeting with
him monthly.** — You don't need a curriculum. You
need a table, a cup of coffee, and the willingness to
share what you've learned. Start this month.

Give something away anonymously this week. —
Money, time, labor — the form doesn't matter. The
anonymity does. Give without anyone knowing. That act
will reveal more about your heart than any public
generosity ever could.

Audit how you spent your last seven days. — Write
down where your hours went. How much went to
screens? How much went to your family? How much
went to purpose? The data will tell you whether you're
living intentionally or drifting. Adjust accordingly.

**Have one conversation this week that you've been
putting off.** — The apology. The truth. The
reconciliation. The confession. Do it this week. Not
because you're ready — because you may not get
another chance.

**Create one family tradition that carries your
values.** — Sunday dinner. A birthday letter. A yearly
camping trip. An annual day of service. Something your
grandchildren will remember and continue. Start it this
month.

Write your own eulogy. — Not as a morbid exercise.
As a compass. Write what you want someone to say

about you at the end. Then read it and ask: "Am I living this right now?" Where the answer is no, you have your marching orders.

Spend one hour this week in silence asking God one question: "What did You make me for?" — No phone. No book. No noise. Just the question and the willingness to listen. Write down whatever comes.

Tell someone you love them today — with your voice, not a screen. — Call them. Or say it face to face. Look them in the eye. Mean every syllable. Don't wait for the right moment. The right moment is now.

CATEGORY 10

FAITH & SPIRITUAL WARFARE

List 1: Ten Ways to Build a Faith That Doesn't Crumble When Life Does

Build it in the calm so it holds in the storm. — The man who waits for the crisis to develop his faith is a man building a boat in the middle of a flood. Faith that survives is faith that was constructed in the ordinary — in the daily prayer, the weekly worship, the regular reading — before the ground started shaking. Build now. The storm is coming. It always is.

Root it in scripture, not in feelings. — Feelings will tell you God has abandoned you. Feelings will tell you the prayer isn't working. Feelings will tell you to quit. Scripture tells you He will never leave you nor forsake you. The man whose faith is anchored to his feelings will be tossed by every wave. The man whose faith is anchored to the Word will stand when the waves come — because the Word doesn't move.

Let doubt refine your faith, not destroy it. — Doubt is not the enemy of faith. Apathy is. The man who wrestles with his belief — who asks the hard questions, who sits in the tension, who refuses to accept easy answers — is building a faith that the man who never questioned his will never have. Wrestling produces strength. Avoidance produces fragility.

Surround yourself with men who believe. — Faith was never meant to be carried alone. You need men who will pray with you, challenge you, and hold you steady when your knees buckle. The man who tries to maintain his faith in isolation will find that isolation erodes everything — including the belief he thought was bulletproof.

Obey before you understand. — Faith is not waiting for clarity before you act. It is acting before clarity arrives — because the One who gave the instruction sees what you cannot. The man who obeys only when he understands has faith in his own comprehension. The man who obeys before he understands has faith in God.

Practice it in the mundane. — Faith is not reserved for the mountaintop moments. It lives in the Tuesday morning prayer. The Wednesday night small group. The Saturday act of service that no one will ever know about. The man who practices faith daily doesn't need to summon it in the crisis. It's already there — because it was never a special occasion. It was a way of life.

Accept that some prayers will not be answered the way you want. — God is not a vending machine. He is a Father. And sometimes the Father says no — not because He doesn't love you, but because He sees something you can't. The man whose faith depends on receiving every answer he wants has a transactional faith. The man whose faith survives the no has a relational one.

Let suffering deepen your faith instead of destroying it. — The deepest wells of faith in history were dug by men in the deepest pain. Not because suffering is good — but because suffering strips away everything that isn't real. And what's left, after the stripping, is either nothing — or God. The man who finds God in the suffering finds a God he could never have found in comfort.

Stay in community even when you want to withdraw. — After loss, after failure, after doubt — the instinct is to pull away from the church, the group, the community. Don't. That's when you need them most. Faith was designed to be held in common. The man who isolates his faith will watch it wither. The man who shares it will watch it survive.

Remember that faith is not certainty — it is trust. — You will not always feel confident. You will not always see the road. You will not always understand the plan. Faith is not the absence of uncertainty. It is the decision to trust the One who holds the future —

even when the present makes no sense. And that decision, made daily, is the strongest foundation a man can stand on.

List 2: Ten Ways to Pray Like a Man Who Actually Believes God Is Listening

Stop performing and start talking. — God doesn't need your theology. He needs your honesty. "God, I'm angry." "God, I'm afraid." "God, I don't know what I'm doing." These are prayers. Real ones. The man who prays with polish is performing. The man who prays with honesty is connecting.

Pray out loud. — There is something about hearing your own voice speak to God that changes the prayer. It moves from thought to declaration. It becomes real in a way that silent prayer sometimes doesn't. You don't need a chapel. Pray in the car. Pray in the shower. Pray walking down the street. Let your voice carry what your heart is holding.

Pray with specifics. — "God, bless my family" is a start. "God, give my wife peace about the diagnosis. Help my son find a friend at school. Give me the courage to have the conversation I've been avoiding" — that's a prayer with teeth. Specific prayers produce specific attention. And specific answers build specific faith.

Pray before you plan. — Most men plan first and pray second — as if God is the backup plan. Reverse it. Before the meeting, before the decision, before the difficult conversation — pray. "God, go ahead of me.

Show me what I can't see." The man who prays first leads differently than the man who prays as an afterthought.

Pray when you don't feel like it. — The morning you're exhausted. The night you're angry. The season you're doubting. Pray anyway. Faithfulness in prayer is not measured by feeling. It is measured by showing up. And the man who prays when he doesn't feel like it is the man who has proven that his faith is not dependent on his mood.

Pray for your enemies. — Not the casual kind. The real kind. The man who wronged you. The boss who fired you. The father who left. Pray for their families. Pray for their growth. Pray for their redemption. It will feel impossible at first. Do it anyway. Something shifts in the heart of a man who prays for the person he wants to hate. Bitterness loosens. Grace moves in.

Pray with your wife. — Not just at meals. Not just at bedtime. Real, vulnerable, honest prayer — kneeling beside her, holding her hand, bringing the marriage before God together. It is the most intimate act available to a husband and wife. And the couples who pray together build a bond that no conflict can sever.

Pray with your children. — Let them hear you talk to God. Let them hear the tremor in your voice. Let them hear you ask for wisdom, confess weakness, and thank God for them by name. A child who hears their father pray learns two things: that God is real, and that their father needs Him. Both of those lessons are priceless.

Keep a record of answered prayers. — Write them down. The job that came through. The relationship that was restored. The fear that was calmed. The provision that arrived. When the next storm comes — and it will — that record becomes your evidence. "He answered before. He will answer again." A prayer journal is not sentimentality. It is ammunition.

Pray like the outcome is already decided — because it is. — God is not surprised by your situation. He is not scrambling to figure out what to do. He is sovereign. He is present. He is working. Pray with the confidence of a man who knows that the outcome is in the hands of someone who has never lost. Not with presumption. With trust. And trust, spoken aloud to God, is the most powerful prayer a man can pray.

List 3: Ten Ways to Read Scripture Like It Was Written for Your Exact Situation

Read it slowly. — The Bible is not a novel to be consumed. It is bread to be chewed. Read a verse. Sit with it. Read it again. Ask what it means. Ask what it demands. The man who reads fast misses the meal. The man who reads slowly is fed.

Ask: "What is God saying to me — right now, today?" — Scripture is not an ancient artifact locked in history. It is alive. Every verse carries the potential to speak directly into the moment you are standing in. Read with the expectation that God has something specific to say to you today. He usually does.

Read the Psalms when you're in pain. — They were written by men who were angry, afraid, grieving, and desperate. They don't sugarcoat. They don't perform.

They scream. They question. They weep. And then —
almost always — they turn to trust. A man in pain who
reads the Psalms will find himself inside them.

Read Proverbs when you need wisdom. — Thirty-
one chapters. One for each day of the month. Every one
packed with practical, direct guidance for money,
relationships, work, speech, and character. A man who
reads one chapter of Proverbs every day for a year will
make decisions differently than the man who doesn't.

Read the Gospels when you've lost your way. —
When you've forgotten what it looks like to live with
purpose, compassion, and courage — go back to Jesus.
Watch how He treated the outcast. Watch how He
confronted the powerful. Watch how He loved the
unlovable. He is the standard. And the man who reads
His story with fresh eyes will find his own path
illuminated.

Memorize what matters most. — Not for
performance. For survival. There will come a moment
when you need a word from God and you don't have a
Bible in your hand. Memorize the verses that have
carried you. Hide them in your heart. They will surface
at exactly the moment you need them — in the hospital
room, in the 2 a.m. darkness, in the middle of the
temptation.

Read with a pen. — Underline. Circle. Write in the
margin. Scripture that is marked up is scripture that
has been engaged with. The Bible was not meant to sit
on a shelf in pristine condition. It was meant to be
worn, stained, bent, and filled with the marks of a man
who has wrestled with its words.

Read it with other men. — A Bible study. A small group. A conversation over coffee. When you read scripture in community, you see things you would have missed alone. Other men bring other eyes — and what one man overlooks, another man catches.

Don't skip the hard parts. — The violence. The judgment. The commands that make you uncomfortable. The stories that don't have happy endings. These are not flaws in the text. They are features. A man who only reads the comfortable parts of scripture is building his faith on half a foundation.

Let it change you. — Reading without application is entertainment. The man who reads, "Love your enemy," and then continues hating his neighbor has not read scripture. He has consumed content. Let the words cost you something. Let them rearrange your schedule, your speech, your relationships. The Bible was not written to inform you. It was written to transform you.

List 4: Ten Ways to Fight the Battles No One Can See

Admit that the war is real. — There is a battle happening inside every man — between discipline and impulse, between integrity and compromise, between faith and fear. Most men deny it. They numb it. They distract themselves from it. But the man who acknowledges the war is the man who can actually fight it.

Guard your mind. — What you consume becomes what you think. What you think becomes what you believe. What you believe becomes what you do. The screen. The content. The voices you listen to. Guard the input — because the output of your life is a direct reflection of what you've allowed into your mind.

Guard your eyes. — The second look. The lingering image. The content you consume when no one is watching. Every man fights this battle. The ones who win are not the ones who never feel the pull. They are the ones who look away. Every time. Without negotiation.

Guard your tongue. — The gossip. The complaint. The cutting remark. The lie you tell to avoid discomfort. Your tongue is a weapon — and in the invisible war, it is either building or destroying. The man who controls his tongue controls the direction of the battle.

Resist the pull of comfort. — Comfort is the quiet enemy. It doesn't attack. It seduces. It whispers, "You deserve a break. You've earned this. One more time won't hurt." And slowly, the man who listens to comfort loses the muscle of discipline. Resist. Not every comfort. But the ones that are slowly making you weaker.

Fast regularly. — From food. From screens. From entertainment. From the thing your flesh craves most. Fasting is the practice of telling your body, "You don't run this. I do." And a man who has authority over his own appetites is a man who has authority in the unseen battle.

Pray the moment the temptation arrives. — Not after. Not later. The moment the pull begins, pray. "God, I need You right now." That prayer is not a magic formula. It is a redirection — from the voice of temptation to the voice of God. And in that redirection, the battle often turns.

Stay accountable. — The man who fights alone loses more often. Find the brother who will ask the hard question every week. "Did you look at it? Did you drink? Did you lie?" Accountability is the human structure God uses to reinforce the spiritual one.

Put on the armor daily. — Truth around your waist. Righteousness on your chest. Peace on your feet. Faith as your shield. Salvation as your helmet. The Word as your sword. These are not metaphors for the casual believer. They are battle gear for the man who knows the war is real and refuses to walk into it naked.

Remember who wins. — The battle is real. The enemy is real. The struggle is real. But the outcome has already been decided. The war has been won by a Man who walked out of a grave. You fight from victory, not toward it. And the man who remembers that fights with a confidence the darkness cannot extinguish.

List 5: Ten Ways to Resist Temptation When You're Tired and Alone

Recognize that tired and alone is the danger zone. — Most men don't fall at their strongest. They fall at their weakest — after the long day, in the empty house, in the late hour when no one is watching and the willpower is gone. Know the pattern. If tired and alone is when you fall, stop being surprised by it and start preparing for it.

Remove yourself from the opportunity. — If the trigger is the screen at midnight, put the screen in another room. If the trigger is the bottle after the family goes to bed, pour it out. If the trigger is the app, delete it. The man who stays in the room with the temptation and relies on willpower is a man who has confused bravery with stupidity.

Call someone. — Before you fall. Not after. Pick up the phone and call the brother who knows your struggle. "I'm in a bad place right now. Talk to me." That sentence breaks the isolation that temptation depends on. And the man who reaches out before the fall is stronger than the man who confesses after it.

Replace the temptation with an action. — When the pull arrives, move. Do pushups. Go for a walk. Open the scripture. Write in a journal. The temptation thrives in passivity. It withers in action. Give your body and your mind something else to do — and the window of vulnerability closes faster than you expect.

Pray the raw prayer. — "God, I want to do the wrong thing right now. I'm too tired to fight this on my own. Help me." That prayer, spoken in the moment of weakness, is the most honest and powerful prayer a man can pray. And God does not ignore the man who comes to Him with empty hands.

Play the tape forward. — You know what happens if you give in. The guilt. The shame. The reset to day one. The look on your wife's face if she knew. Play the full tape — not just the first five minutes of relief, but the hours and days that follow. The temporary pleasure is never worth the permanent cost.

Get off the device. — Most modern temptation is delivered through a screen. If you're tired and alone and holding a device, you are holding the delivery mechanism. Put it down. In another room. Face down is not enough. Out of reach is the minimum. The man who removes the device removes the portal.

Go to sleep. — Sometimes the most spiritual thing you can do is close your eyes. Fatigue lowers every defense. And the man who goes to bed at ten instead of staying up until midnight has just avoided the hours where most men fall. Sleep is not avoidance. It is strategy.

Remember your identity. — You are not the man the temptation tells you to be. You are a man of God. A husband. A father. A man who has been bought with a price. The temptation says, "This is who you really are." The truth says, "This is who you used to be." Stand on the truth. Even when the lie is louder.

Get back up if you fall. — You may fail tonight. If you do, get up tomorrow. Confess it. Grieve it. Learn from it. And fight again. The man who falls and stays down has been defeated. The man who falls and rises has simply stumbled on the road to freedom. The battle is not over until you quit fighting. Don't quit.

List 6: Ten Ways to Forgive Yourself for the Man You Used to Be

Stop punishing yourself for what the blood already covered. — If God has forgiven you, your self-punishment is not righteousness. It is arrogance — the belief that your standard is higher than His. He said it is finished. Believe Him.

Separate who you were from who you are becoming. — The man who drank. The man who lied. The man who abandoned. That was then. This is now. You are not sentenced to the identity of your worst season. You are a man in process — and process means change is not just possible. It's happening.

Name what you did without minimizing or amplifying. — Don't dismiss it: "It wasn't that bad." And don't catastrophize it: "I'm the worst man who ever lived." Name it honestly. "I did this. It was wrong. It cost people I love." Honest naming is the bridge between shame and healing.

Make the amends you can — and release the ones you can't. — If the person is reachable, apologize. If the damage is repairable, repair it. But if the person is gone, if the moment has passed, if the bridge has burned beyond rebuilding — release it. You cannot undo what is done. You can only live differently from this point forward.

Stop replaying the highlight reel of your failures. — Your mind will loop the worst moments on repeat if you let it. Every loop deepens the shame. At some point, you must press stop — not because the failure doesn't matter, but because the replay is preventing the man you're becoming from showing up.

Receive the grace that you extend to others. — You would forgive your son. You would forgive your friend. You would tell any man on earth that his past does not define him. Now say it to yourself. The same grace you give away is the same grace available to you. Stop being the one person you refuse to extend it to.

Let the scar be a teacher, not a torturer. — The scar exists. It will always exist. But its purpose is not to punish you forever. Its purpose is to remind you where you've been — so you never go back. A scar that teaches makes the man wiser. A scar that tortures keeps the man imprisoned.

Do the next right thing. — Self-forgiveness is not an emotion you arrive at. It is a direction you walk in. And the direction is forward. The next right decision. The next honest conversation. The next kept promise. Each one is a brick in the bridge between the man you were and the man you are becoming.

Tell someone who you used to be — and let them love you anyway. — The shame says, "If they knew, they'd leave." The truth is, the people who know your worst and stay are the people who love you for real. Let them in. Let them hold the story with you. Their acceptance is the mirror that shows you what God's forgiveness looks like in human form.

Let God finish the work He started. — He who began a good work in you will carry it on to completion. You are not finished. You are not disqualified. You are mid-construction. And the Architect who started the project doesn't abandon it because of a cracked wall. He repairs it. He strengthens it. And He finishes it. Let Him.

List 7: Ten Ways to Trust God When He's Silent

Accept that silence is not absence. — The doctor is silent while performing surgery. The teacher is silent while the student takes the test. Silence does not mean God has left the room. It often means He is doing something that requires your patience, not His explanation.

Read what He has already said. — When the new word from God hasn't arrived, return to the old one. Scripture is not outdated because your situation is new. The promises He made three thousand years ago are as binding today as the day they were spoken. When heaven is quiet, the Bible is not.

Obey the last thing He told you. — Most men are asking God for the next instruction while ignoring the last one. If He told you to forgive, forgive. If He told you to give, give. If He told you to stay, stay. New direction comes after obedience to the current one.

Wait without wandering. — The silence tempts you to find your own answer. To take control. To fill the void with action that looks productive but is really just impatience. Resist. Wait. Not passively — expectantly. The man who waits well receives what the man who runs ahead misses.

Pour into the things you can control. — While you wait for God to speak about the future, work on the present. Strengthen your marriage. Serve your community. Deepen your faith. Build your body. Silence is not a season of inactivity. It is a season of preparation.

Look for Him in the ordinary. — God doesn't always speak in thunder. Sometimes He speaks through the friend who calls at the right moment. The verse that jumps off the page. The peace that arrives for no reason. The door that opens when you weren't looking. Train yourself to see Him in the small things — because in the silent seasons, the small things are where He's most active.

Recall what He did last time. — He was silent before the promotion. He was silent before the healing. He was silent before the answer that changed everything. And then He moved. He will move again. The record of past faithfulness is the fuel for present trust.

Stay in community. — The silent season is when isolation becomes most dangerous. Don't withdraw from the men who walk with you. Let them carry your faith when you can't carry it yourself. That's what brothers are for.

Tell Him how you feel. — "God, I can't hear You. I'm confused. I'm frustrated. I need You to show up." He can handle your honesty. He prefers it. The man who tells God the truth about his struggle is closer to God than the man who performs contentment he doesn't feel.

Trust the silence itself as part of the plan. — The silence is not a mistake. It is not a delay. It is not a punishment. It is a tool — the tool God uses to build a faith that doesn't need constant confirmation to survive. The man who trusts God in the silence has a faith that noise can never shake.

List 8: Ten Ways to Lead Your Family Spiritually Without Faking It

Start imperfectly. — The reason most men never lead their families spiritually is because they're waiting to feel qualified. You will never feel qualified. Start anyway. A stumbling prayer at the dinner table is infinitely better than a polished silence.

Pray with your family out loud. — Not eloquent prayers. Honest ones. "God, thank You for this food. Help us love each other well today. Forgive me where I fell short." Your family doesn't need a pastor. They need a father who talks to God like He's in the room — because He is.

Read scripture together. — Even five minutes. Even one verse. The man who reads the Bible with his family — at dinner, at bedtime, on the drive to school — is depositing truth into their lives that will surface decades later in moments he'll never witness.

Admit what you don't know. — "I don't understand this verse. Let's look it up together." "I'm not sure what God is doing right now, but I trust Him." Spiritual leadership is not having all the answers. It is modeling the pursuit of them.

Let them see you on your knees. — Not as a performance. As a lifestyle. The child who sees their father kneeling in prayer learns something no Sunday school can teach: that the strongest man they know is not too strong to bow.

Apologize when you fail spiritually. — "I lost my temper, and that wasn't Christlike. I'm sorry." "I haven't been leading us well in this area, and I want to do better." A man who confesses his spiritual failures to his family teaches them that faith is not perfection. It is pursuit.

Serve the church, not just attend it. — Your family is watching whether church is something you consume or something you contribute to. Volunteer. Serve. Show up early. Stay late. A father who serves the church raises children who see faith as active, not passive.

Talk about God in normal conversation. — Not just at church. At the dinner table. In the car. On the walk. "I think God is teaching me something about patience." "I was reading this morning and it reminded me of what we're going through." When God is part of the daily conversation, faith becomes part of the daily life.

Protect your family from spiritual threats. — The content that contradicts your values. The relationships that erode your faith. The cultural messages that undermine what you're building. Spiritual leadership includes standing guard — not in paranoia, but in wisdom.

Be consistent. — The family devotion that happens every Tuesday is more powerful than the spiritual marathon that happens once a year. Consistency communicates commitment. And commitment is the foundation your family's faith is built on.

List 9: Ten Ways to Worship Through Suffering Instead of Running from It

Acknowledge the pain to God — without editing it. — "God, this hurts. I don't understand it. I'm angry. I'm scared." That's worship. Not because it sounds worshipful — but because it is honest. And honesty before God is the purest form of worship available to a suffering man.

Choose gratitude as an act of war. — In the middle of the suffering, name one thing you're grateful for. Then another. Gratitude in suffering is not denial. It is defiance — a declaration that the darkness has not consumed everything. And that declaration, spoken from the pit, is worship.

Sing when you don't feel like singing. — The hymn through the tears. The worship song in the hospital room. The praise that comes from a broken man. These are the offerings that move heaven — not because they're beautiful, but because they're costly. Worship that costs nothing is worth nothing.

Serve someone in worse condition than you. — Worship is not just vertical. It is horizontal. The man who serves another person's suffering while carrying his own has made his pain an altar. And on that altar, something sacred happens.

Stay in the community of faith. — Don't withdraw from the church. Don't stop showing up. The community that gathers around a suffering man and worships with him creates a sound that the man alone could never produce.

Let the suffering strip you down to what's real. — Suffering removes the excess. The pride. The pretense. The performance. And what's left is the raw, undecorated soul standing before God with nothing to offer but itself. That offering — naked, trembling, honest — is the most authentic worship a man can bring.

Read Job. — The man who lost everything and still said, "Though He slay me, yet will I trust in Him." Job didn't worship because he understood. He worshipped because he trusted. And the man who reads Job in the middle of his own suffering finds a companion and a model.

Refuse to curse God. — You will be tempted. The pain will feel unjust. The silence will feel cruel. And the voice inside you will say, "He doesn't care." Refuse it. Not because the pain isn't real. Because God is bigger than the pain. And the man who refuses to curse God in the fire is the man who walks out of it refined.

Let the suffering produce something. — Empathy. Depth. Compassion. Patience. Wisdom. The man who walks through suffering with his eyes open walks out carrying gifts that the comfortable man will never possess. These gifts are the fruit of worship in the fire.

Trust that He is with you in it. — Not above it. Not watching from a distance. With you. In the hospital

room. In the courtroom. In the grief. In the silence.
"Even though I walk through the valley of the shadow
of death, I will fear no evil, for You are with me." That's
not poetry. That's a promise. And the man who believes
it has found the deepest form of worship available to
the human soul.

List 10: Ten Ways to Stand on the Word When the World Tells You It's Outdated

Know what it says. — You cannot defend a book you
haven't read. The world dismisses the Bible because it
counts on your ignorance. Read it. Study it. Know what
it says and why. The man who knows the Word is not
intimidated by the man who mocks it.

Understand that unpopular does not mean untrue.
— The Word has always been countercultural. It was
countercultural when it was written, and it is
countercultural now. That is not a flaw. That is a
feature. Truth does not change because the culture
does. The man who stands on the Word stands on
something the culture can never erode.

Let your life be the argument. — The most
persuasive defense of scripture is not a debate. It is a
life. A marriage that lasts. A man who keeps his word.
A father who is present. A friend who forgives. The
world may dismiss the Book — but it cannot dismiss the
man whose life was transformed by it.

Don't argue — live. — You will not win the Twitter
debate. You will not convince the mocker with a
paragraph. But you can live with such integrity, such

love, such discipline, that the people around you stop arguing with the Book and start asking about the Author.

Teach it to your children before the world teaches them otherwise. — The world will present its case — loudly, persuasively, relentlessly. If your children don't know what the Word says before that case is made, they will have no foundation to evaluate it. Teach them young. Teach them often. Teach them why.

Accept the cost. — Standing on the Word will cost you friendships. It may cost you promotions. It will cost you cultural approval. Accept the cost before it arrives — so that when it does, you've already decided what you're willing to pay.

Hold the Word with conviction and the person with compassion. — You can hold the truth without holding contempt. You can disagree without dehumanizing. The man who stands on the Word with a clenched fist has missed the entire point of the Word. Hold the Book firmly. Hold the person gently. Both are required.

Study the men who stood before you. — The martyrs. The reformers. The fathers of the faith. They stood on the Word when standing meant prison, exile, or death. Your discomfort is not their sacrifice — but their example is your fuel.

Expect the ridicule — and don't let it move you. — They laughed at Noah. They mocked the prophets. They crucified the Savior. Ridicule is not evidence that you're wrong. It is evidence that you're standing on something the world cannot control. Let them laugh. You're not building for their applause.

Stand on it not because it's easy, but because it's true. — The Word of God is not a suggestion. It is not a cultural relic. It is not a book of outdated moralism. It is the living, breathing, active Word of the God who spoke the universe into existence. And the man who stands on it — quietly, firmly, without apology — is standing on the only thing that will still be standing when everything else has fallen.

FAITH & SPIRITUAL WARFARE: QUOTES

"Be on your guard; stand firm in the faith; be courageous; be strong." — 1 Corinthians 16:13

"The Lord is my shepherd; I shall not want." — Psalm 23:1

"For our struggle is not against flesh and blood, but against the rulers, against the authorities, against the powers of this dark world and against the spiritual forces of evil in the heavenly realms." — Ephesians 6:12

"Trust in the Lord with all your heart and lean not on your own understanding; in all your ways submit to him, and he will make your paths straight." — Proverbs 3:5-6

"I can do all things through Christ who strengthens me." — Philippians 4:13

"Have I not commanded you? Be strong and courageous. Do not be afraid; do not be discouraged, for the Lord your God will be with you wherever you go." — Joshua 1:9

"The prayer of a righteous person is powerful and effective." — James 5:16

"But those who hope in the Lord will renew their strength. They will soar on wings like eagles; they will run and not grow weary, they will walk and not be faint." — Isaiah 40:31

"Submit yourselves, then, to God. Resist the devil, and he will flee from you." — James 4:7

"For the word of God is alive and active. Sharper than any double-edged sword, it penetrates even to dividing soul and spirit, joints and marrow; it judges the thoughts and attitudes of the heart." — Hebrews 4:12

FAITH & SPIRITUAL WARFARE: PUTTING IT INTO PRACTICE

Read one chapter of Proverbs every day this month. — Thirty-one chapters for thirty-one days. One per day. Let the wisdom accumulate. By month's end, you will think differently — not because you tried to, but because the Word did its work.

Pray out loud with your family once this week. — At dinner. At bedtime. Before school. Wherever. Not a perfect prayer — a real one. Let them hear your voice talking to God.

Memorize one verse this week. — Write it on a card. Put it in your pocket. Read it ten times a day. By

Friday, it will be in your heart. And it will surface when you need it most.

Identify your spiritual danger zone — tired, alone, late at night — and build a plan for it. — Remove the device. Set the alarm. Call the friend. The man who plans for the danger zone survives it.

Fast from one thing this week as an act of spiritual discipline. — A meal. A screen. A comfort. Let the hunger remind you that your body does not run your life. Your spirit does.

Write down three prayers God has already answered. — Keep the list. Add to it. When doubt arrives, read it. Evidence of past faithfulness is the strongest foundation for present trust.

Find one man and ask him to hold you spiritually accountable. — "Ask me every week if I'm reading. If I'm praying. If I'm fighting the battles no one can see." Invite the accountability. Then don't flinch when it comes.

Attend a worship service this week — even if you don't feel like it. — Especially if you don't feel like it. Worship in the drought is the worship that moves mountains.

Confess one hidden struggle to God and to one trusted person. — Out loud. In full. Not the edited version. The full truth. Freedom lives on the other side of that sentence.

Before you go to sleep tonight, tell God one thing you're grateful for and one thing you need. —

That's a complete prayer. Gratitude and need. Start there. Do it every night this week. Watch what shifts.

CONCLUSION

You have read one hundred lists. One thousand truths. Ten categories that touch every corner of a man's life.

Now the question is simple: what will you do with them?

You can close this book, nod in agreement, and return to the same patterns that brought you here. You can bookmark the pages that convicted you and never open them again. You can share a quote on the internet and never apply it in your kitchen.

Or you can do what this book was written for: become the man you were always meant to be.

Not the man the culture wants you to be. Not the man your father failed to show you. Not the man the screen tells you to admire. The man God designed when He formed you — the one with strength enough to lead and humility enough to serve, with hands strong enough to protect and gentle enough to hold, with a voice loud enough to speak truth and quiet enough to listen.

That man is not a myth. He is not an impossibility. He is a decision — made daily, tested constantly, and refined by every storm that comes.

Start today. Pick one list. Apply one item. Tell one person what you read. Write one letter. Make one call. Pray one prayer.

The forgotten standards were never lost. They were abandoned. And they have been waiting — patiently, quietly, eternally — for the man who has the courage to pick them back up.

Be that man.

APPENDIX A: SCRIPTURE FOUNDATIONS

The following passages form the biblical bedrock of the standards in this book. They are not decorations. They are the foundation. Read them slowly. Memorize the ones that pierce you. Return to them when the world tells you they're outdated.

On Manhood & Identity: 1 Corinthians 16:13 • Micah 6:8 • Psalm 1:1-3 • Jeremiah 17:7-8

On Brotherhood: Proverbs 27:17 • Ecclesiastes 4:9-12 • Proverbs 17:17 • John 15:13

On Fatherhood: Proverbs 22:6 • Ephesians 6:4 • Deuteronomy 6:6-7 • Psalm 127:3-5

On Marriage & Devotion: Ephesians 5:25-28 • 1 Corinthians 13:4-7 • Proverbs 18:22 • Mark 10:9

On Leadership: Mark 10:43-45 • Matthew 23:11 • Proverbs 29:18 • Joshua 24:15

On Work & Provision: Colossians 3:23-24 • Proverbs 10:4 • 2 Thessalonians 3:10 • Proverbs 16:3

On Physical Discipline: 1 Corinthians 6:19-20 • 1 Corinthians 9:27 • Romans 12:1 • 3 John 1:2

On Mental Toughness: James 1:2-4 • 2 Corinthians 4:8-9 • Romans 5:3-5 • Isaiah 40:31

On Legacy & Purpose: Proverbs 13:22 • Ephesians 2:10 • 2 Timothy 4:7 • Micah 6:8

On Faith & Spiritual Warfare: Ephesians 6:10-18 • James 4:7 • Hebrews 4:12 • Proverbs 3:5-6

APPENDIX B: RECOMMENDED READING

Wild at Heart by John Eldredge *The Man in the Mirror* by Patrick Morley *Kingdom Man* by Tony Evans *Disciplines of a Godly Man* by R. Kent Hughes *Mere Christianity* by C.S. Lewis *The Screwtape Letters* by C.S. Lewis *Boundaries* by Henry Cloud and John Townsend *The 7 Habits of Highly Effective People* by Stephen R. Covey *Man's Search for Meaning* by Viktor E. Frankl *Proverbs* (the entire book — read monthly)

APPENDIX C: COMPLETE INDEX OF LISTS

Category 1: Manhood & Identity List 1: Ten Marks of a Man Who Knows Who He Is List 2: Ten Lies the World Tells Men About Masculinity List 3: Ten Ways to Define Yourself Before the World Does It for You List 4: Ten Things Every Man Should Know by the Time He's Thirty List 5: Ten Ways to Be Strong Without Being

Dangerous List 6: Ten Ways to Be Gentle Without Being Weak List 7: Ten Ways to Kill the Boy and Let the Man Live List 8: Ten Standards Every Man Should Refuse to Lower List 9: Ten Ways to Stop Performing and Start Being List 10: Ten Ways to Carry Yourself with Quiet Confidence

Category 2: Brotherhood List 1: Ten Ways to Build Friendships That Will Save Your Life List 2: Ten Things a Real Friend Will Do That a Fake One Never Will List 3: Ten Ways to Be the Friend Every Man Needs but Few Have List 4: Ten Ways to Have the Hard Conversation Instead of Walking Away List 5: Ten Ways to Show Up for Another Man Without Being Asked List 6: Ten Ways to Hold Another Man Accountable Without Destroying the Relationship List 7: Ten Ways to Forgive a Brother Who Let You Down List 8: Ten Ways to Build a Circle That Sharpens You List 9: Ten Ways to Be Vulnerable Without Losing Respect List 10: Ten Ways to Recognize When You're Isolated and What to Do About It

Category 3: Fatherhood List 1: Ten Things Your Children Need from You More Than Money List 2: Ten Ways to Raise a Son Who Becomes a Good Man List 3: Ten Ways to Raise a Daughter Who Knows Her Worth List 4: Ten Ways to Discipline Without Destroying List 5: Ten Ways to Stay Present When Your Work Demands Everything List 6: Ten Things to Teach Your Children Before They Leave Your House List 7: Ten Ways to Repair the Damage When You've Failed as a Father List 8: Ten Ways to Be the Father You Never Had List 9: Ten Ways to Lead Your Family Through Crisis List 10: Ten Ways to Let Your Children See the Real You

Category 4: Marriage & Devotion List 1: Ten Ways to Love Your Wife Like She's the Only Woman in the World List 2: Ten Things That Will Destroy Your Marriage If You Let Them List 3: Ten Ways to Fight Fair and Never Fight Dirty List 4: Ten Ways to Protect Your Marriage from the Outside List 5: Ten Ways to Lead Your Home Without Controlling It List 6: Ten Ways to Be Emotionally Available When Everything in You Wants to Shut Down List 7: Ten Ways to Rebuild Trust After You've Broken It List 8: Ten Ways to Keep the Fire Alive After the Honeymoon Ends List 9: Ten Ways to Honor Your Wife in Public and in Private List 10: Ten Ways to Be the Husband She Deserves Even When You Don't Feel Like It

Category 5: Leadership List 1: Ten Ways to Lead When Nobody Gave You Permission List 2: Ten Ways to Earn Respect Without Demanding It List 3: Ten Ways to Make Decisions That Protect the People You Lead List 4: Ten Ways to Admit You Were Wrong and Still Lead Forward List 5: Ten Ways to Lead Under Pressure Without Breaking List 6: Ten Ways to Raise Up Other Leaders Instead of Building a Kingdom Around Yourself List 7: Ten Ways to Stand Alone When the Crowd Goes the Other Way List 8: Ten Ways to Lead with Integrity When Cutting Corners Would Be Easier List 9: Ten Ways to Handle Power Without Letting It Handle You List 10: Ten Ways to Serve the People You Lead Rather Than Use Them

Category 6: Work & Provision List 1: Ten Ways to Work Like It Matters Even When Nobody's Watching List 2: Ten Ways to Provide for Your Family Without Losing Your Soul List 3: Ten Ways to Build a

Reputation That Opens Doors You Never Knocked On List 4: Ten Ways to Handle a Job You Hate with a Character Worth Respecting List 5: Ten Ways to Be the Hardest Worker in the Room Without Making It Your Identity List 6: Ten Ways to Deal with Failure at Work Without Letting It Follow You Home List 7: Ten Ways to Treat Money as a Tool and Not a Trophy List 8: Ten Ways to Mentor a Younger Man in Your Workplace List 9: Ten Ways to Start Over When Everything You Built Falls Apart List 10: Ten Ways to Leave a Workplace Better Than You Found It

Category 7: Physical Discipline List 1: Ten Ways to Train Your Body Like a Man Who Respects the Gift List 2: Ten Ways to Build Discipline That Lasts Beyond the Gym List 3: Ten Ways to Eat Like You Give a Damn About Your Future List 4: Ten Ways to Rest Without Guilt and Work Without Burnout List 5: Ten Ways to Break an Addiction That's Been Breaking You List 6: Ten Ways to Age Strong Instead of Just Getting Old List 7: Ten Ways to Stop Treating Your Body Like It's Disposable List 8: Ten Ways to Build Endurance for the Long Fights in Life List 9: Ten Ways to Show Up Physically for the People Who Depend on You List 10: Ten Ways to Compete with Yourself Instead of Comparing Yourself to Others

Category 8: Mental Toughness List 1: Ten Ways to Endure Pain Without Becoming Bitter List 2: Ten Ways to Control Your Emotions Before They Control You List 3: Ten Ways to Stay Focused When Everything Around You Is Noise List 4: Ten Ways to Handle Rejection Like a Man Who Knows His Value List 5: Ten Ways to Think Clearly Under Pressure List 6: Ten Ways to Rebuild

Your Mind After Trauma or Loss List 7: Ten Ways to Stop Living in Fear of What Might Happen List 8: Ten Ways to Silence the Voice That Tells You You're Not Enough List 9: Ten Ways to Be Patient When Everything in You Wants to Quit List 10: Ten Ways to Find Peace in the Middle of the Storm

Category 9: Legacy & Purpose List 1: Ten Ways to Live for Something Bigger Than Yourself List 2: Ten Ways to Build Something That Will Outlast You List 3: Ten Ways to Find Your Purpose When the World Says You Don't Have One List 4: Ten Ways to Leave a Legacy That Has Nothing to Do with Money List 5: Ten Ways to Write a Story with Your Life That's Worth Telling List 6: Ten Ways to Invest in the Next Generation When No One Invested in You List 7: Ten Ways to Live with Urgency Without Living with Anxiety List 8: Ten Ways to Measure Your Life by What You Gave, Not What You Got List 9: Ten Ways to Make Every Year Count After Forty List 10: Ten Ways to Die with Nothing Left Undone and Nothing Left Unsaid

Category 10: Faith & Spiritual Warfare List 1: Ten Ways to Build a Faith That Doesn't Crumble When Life Does List 2: Ten Ways to Pray Like a Man Who Actually Believes God Is Listening List 3: Ten Ways to Read Scripture Like It Was Written for Your Exact Situation List 4: Ten Ways to Fight the Battles No One Can See List 5: Ten Ways to Resist Temptation When You're Tired and Alone List 6: Ten Ways to Forgive Yourself for the Man You Used to Be List 7: Ten Ways to Trust God When He's Silent List 8: Ten Ways to Lead Your Family Spiritually Without Faking It List 9: Ten Ways to Worship Through Suffering Instead of Running from It

List 10: Ten Ways to Stand on the Word When the World Tells You It's Outdated

www.ingramcontent.com/pod-product-compliance
Lightning Source LLC
Chambersburg PA
CBHW020334180726
47991CB00020B/1573